SIMPLE REFORMS FOR A BETTER SOCIETY

SIMPLE REFORMS FOR A BETTER SOCIETY

N. RAMANADHA RAO

Foreword by
SADIQ ALI

GYAN PUBLISHING HOUSE
NEW DELHI-110002

SIMPLE REFORMS FOR A BETTER SOCIETY
(*Social & Political Reforms*)

ISBN : 81-212-0479-8

Published in 1998 in India by
Gyan Publishing House
5, Ansari Road
New Delhi-110 002

Laser Type Setting at Blossoms, New Delhi
Printed at Mehra Offset Press, New Delhi

This book is dedicated to the memory of my father,
Shri NAMAGIRI NARAYANA MURTY

N. RAMANADHA RAO

Contents

Foreword

Shri N. Ramanadha Rao was good enough to ask me to write a foreword to this book. Being otherwise busy, I showed reluctance, but, when I went through the book in manuscript or rather a considerable portion of it, I found myself attracted by its contents. It contains interesting and at times illuminating observations on several aspects of the current political, social and economic situation in the country. I was a little astonished at the wide range of interests cultivated by Shri Rao, who is an Engineer, by profession. But, of course, occasionally we do come across people like him whose interests extend beyond their fields of specialization and as good citizens, they take interest in things around them and matters which concern the well-being of the common people.

When India became independent fifty years ago, we all thought that in the years to follow the entire tough and harsh problems that faced the country would be on their way out gradually, with effective solutions found for them. No doubt, advances have been made in several directions, but we see that apart from many old problems, some new ones have also arisen. We wished to be at peace with the world and yet we have now to contend with more dangers to peace than in the earlier days of our independence. Poverty, unemployment and much else continue to be sources of serious and wide spread anxiety. Our politics are by no means of a high order even though; some features of our polity fill us with hope and save us from despair. We also cannot claim that our vast administrative structure is reasonably clean and efficient. As we look around, we encounter a plethora of problems, quite a few of which Shri Rao has touched in the pages that follow. He has described and analyzed each problem in the brief compass that the book permits and suggested the lines on which solutions should be worked out. Anyone interested in this particular topic will find Shri Rao's study, a useful reading.

New Delhi
3.3.98

SADIQ ALI
Chairman, Gandhi Smarak Nidhi
(Former Governor of Maharashtra)

Preface

Striving for a better society is in fact, a constant and continuing endeavour of the people ever since the dawn of civilization.

Several social reformers have appeared on the scene from time to time and brought about radical changes in some of the customs and beliefs, which were oppressing large sections of the people.

Monarchy and autocracy have yielded place to democracy in many countries after a few revolutions and social upheavals.

Industry, Science and Technology have brought many material comforts within the reach of the people. Great thinkers and saintly persons have been preaching to work for harmony and happiness of all the people. In spite of all this, the society is still beset with many problems.

Many people are still being oppressed and exploited. The disparities between the rich and the poor are increasing, day by day.

Common people are unable to seek judicial remedies for the injustices suffered by them because of the exhorbitant cost and delay involved.

Illiteracy is hampering the development of human resources to their full potential. Educational reforms carried out from time to time have not yet achieved the desired results.

Democracy is being subverted by the vested interests. Corruption and criminalisation of politics have made the lives of the common people miserable. The rules are complicated and are often bent to suit the needs of the privileged people.

Formation of too many political parties, unseemly quarrels between them, lack of a proper direction in the absence of great and dedicated leaders and the instability of the Governments are causing a great deal of concern to the thinking public.

In this book, I have made a humble attempt to pin point some of the problems and suggested a few simple remedies. I sincerely hope that this book should contribute to (1) the thinking of the people on the problems of the day, (2) setting in motion a healthy debate, and (3) finding solutions to suit the present times.

I would like to express my thanks to Sri G. Gundaiah, Managing Director, Rani Constructions Pvt. Ltd. New Delhi - 110058 for having borne the expenses of printing this book. I appreciate him whole heartedly for the interest he has evinced in the subjects dealt with in this book.

N. RAMANADHA RAO

1

Fifty Years of Independence An Introspection

August 15 of 1947 stands out as a most memorable day in the history of our country. The independence that we have attained on that day is indeed priceless. That our country's sovereignty and integrity are preserved in these fifty years is itself a good enough reason to celebrate the golden jubilee of our independence on a grand scale. However, a thorough introspection is also needed on this occasion to pinpoint the areas in which a special effort is needed in the next few years to make the people happy and contented.

With the attainment of independence, the expectations and aspirations of the people rose very high. The leaders promised that the political revolution would be followed by an economic and social revolution. But this promise is yet to be kept up in the form that satisfies the people.

Gandhiji said, "By political independence, I do not mean an imitation of the House of Commons or the Soviet rule in Russia or the Fascist rule of Italy or the Nazi rule of Germany. They have systems suited to their genius. We must have ours to suit ours. I have described it as Ram raj". If Ramraj means a land of prosperity and justice where the people are well satisfied and happy and free from wants, we must admit that we are still nowhere near that goal.

For, more than one third of the population is still below the poverty line. Millions of people are remaining unemployed.

Despite the frequent calls for the elimination of child labour, hundreds of thousands of children are working in various industries and workshops, including those of hazardous nature for earning their livelihood. They cannot afford to go to school because of their conditions of poverty. Schemes for the removal of illiteracy have not made much headway. The crime rate as well as the police atrocities are increasing day by day. Common man is losing confidence in the judicial system because of the inordinate delay in disposal of cases, the exhorbitant cost involved, and some times what appears to be a miscarriage of justice.

The essential commodities are often found to be scarce. The prices are constantly rising. The disparities between the rich and the poor are widening to an alarming degree.

Corruption has seeped into all sections of the society. Selfishness has become the order of the day. Money power is over shadowing moral strength. Even social service is being subtly converted into commercial enterprise. Those in change of such organisations are openly running after power, money and honours.

It is not intended here to say that the country has not developed at all. Many steel plants, cement plants, fertiliser plants, automobile factories, thermal and hydel power houses and several other industries have been set up in the last fifty years. Many educational institutions, universities and premier research stations have come into existence. Several dams, bridges, highways etc. have also been constructed.

But we have not attained self sufficiency in any of the vital areas. For setting up of most of the industries, we are still very much dependent on foreign technology, foreign machines and foreign technicians. Due to several avoidable causes, the setting up of these industries and implementation of other development projects are usually getting delayed and costing much more than the optimum cost. Moreover, the defective operation and faulty management are resulting in low production and poor quality in many of the factories. The public distribution system is far from satisfactory.

The power supply in rural areas is totally unreliable. Even in towns and cities, there are innumerable power cuts all through the year. The buses are over-crowded. Slums and pollution are proving to be a menace in cities. Abnormal delays and inefficiency have become quite common in Government offices.

It is in such circumstances that people start comparing the conditions in India with those in other countries. For instance, Japan and Germany were shattered in the second world war which ended just two years before we attained our independence. Those countries have rebuilt their economy and industry at such a spectacular rate that they are today competing with the most advanced countries like the U.S., the U.K. and France. About 50 years ago the countries like China, Malaysia, Indonesia and Thailand were more are less in the same condition as India was. But, today they are way ahead of us in per capita income and the general living conditions of the people.

Perhaps, independent India made a good beginning under the leadership of Jawaharlal Nehru. His advocacy of the principles of democracy and secularism and his commitment to usher in a socialistic society had enthused the people a great deal. The five year plans initiated by him on the Soviet pattern held out the prospect of rapid development of the country.

But, the implementation of his domestic policies suffered to a large extent because of several problems which are normally faced by any newly-independent country. Apart from this, the three main causes which have hampered the economic progress are (i) corruption, (ii) an alarming growth of population and (iii) the three wars that India had to fight, two against Pakistan and one against China.

Some parties and leaders are following the policy of coming to power by hook or the crook. At the drop of the hat, they are switching their loyalty from one party to another. Some of them are forming alliances without any principles at all.

The object of the parties in formulating their policies seems to be to woo the voters of one group or a caste or a community rather than their conviction that they would serve the larger cause of the Nation as a whole.

Generally, politicians are respected as they are supposed to seek power to serve the interests of the people. Therefore, their salaries are also comparatively low. But, now-a-days, the politicians seem to seek power for their own personal benefit. Most of them have become unduly rich after taking up politics as a profession, leaving the people they are supposed to serve in stark poverty and miserable conditions.

If indeed, the development of the country could be achieved through speeches and pious platitudes of the politicians, our country would have become by now one of the most advanced countries. For, most of the politicians are making several promises in their speeches for improving the condition of the people. But they seldom keep up those promises.

The debates in the Parliament and State legislatures are often turning acrimonious. The members are making allegations of corruption, malpractices and improprieties against one another.

The instability of Governments, the many scams that have come to light and weak leadership are leading to unhealthy trends taking root in the polity. The journalists are taking the role of investigating agencies. The judiciary seems to be making forays into the executive's role. Constitutional authorities like the Election Commission are behaving as through they are not bothered about the Government.

The legislators are often causing embarrassment to the Government and other constitutional authorities by their actions and utterances, being protected by their privilege of immunity. The country's democracy can be preserved only when the Legislature, the Executive, the Judiciary and the fourth estate work within bounds of their respective areas.

The news of the leaders and parties cover more about their

clashes and quarrels than about their efforts for development of the country. In fact, the people are deriving a lot of entertain ment by reading the news about them; now-a-days.

The people would have appreciated the leaders, if they had set for themselves the goal of converting at least 50 villages as model villages provided wi th all amenities like protected drinking water supply, electricity, a school, a hospital, pucca roads, good sanitary conditions in every State by the time these celebrations are held. Alas, the conditions in the villages are still very miserable. Let the leaders resolve on this occasion to transform the villages into healthy living places with all amenities at least by the time the diamond jubilee celebrations are held in the year 2007.

2

What People Expect of Stable Governments

Setting at nought the many speculations about a possible mid-term poll, the Narasimha Rao Government had completed its full term of five years, as it was being assured repeatedly by the Prime Minister from the beginning.

His Government had survived many crises such as those emanating from the demolition of the Babri Masjid, the serial bomb blasts in Bombay, the securities scam, several corruption charges, defeat of the Congress Party in the Assembly elections in Andhra Pradesh, Karnataka, Maharashtra, Gujarat and Bihar and the split in the party caused by Arjun Singh.

The main advantages of a stable government are that it gives time to the government to fulfil its party's election promises and it avoids the expenditure involved in a mid-term poll. An unstable and short-lived government often gets away with excuses for its failure to keep up its promises. But a stable government remaining in office for its full term cannot escape blame if it fails to perform as per the expectations aroused by it.

In the wake of the Central Government's liberalisation of the industrial and economic policy, the salaries of the top management personnel have increased many-fold and the profits of the people in business have also gone up substantially on account of the tax benefits and other incentives given to them. But the condition of the vast majority of the people working at lower rungs has not improved at all in spite of a marginal increase in their wages as it is more or less offset by the steep rise in prices. As a result, the disparity between the upper strata and the lower strata has become far wider now. The people are surely more concerned about their economic well being than any other issue.

The election promises like creating one crore of new jobs and construction of a million houses for the poor have mostly remained unfulfilled. The much publicised schemes for the elimination of child labour and removal of illiteracy have also not made much headway. The reason for the children seeking employment and the parents not sending them to schools is obviously their poverty.

Therefore, alternative source of income should be provided to the families of those children. These schemes should be taken up industry wise or area wise in stages and should be implemented in the whole of the country in a definite time frame of ten years or so. The details of implementation and the results achieved should be reported to the Parliament once in a year.

The people's representatives and the elected governments are unable to check the rampant corruption, as very often they themselves are found guilty of corrupt practices. Some people have made a fortune in politics or business within a very short time of 10 to 15 years after having started their careers from a scratch.

Stringent measures should be taken to scrutinise the source of their income and confiscate the illegally amassed wealth and award a deterrant punishment to such offenders. Only then, the confidence of the people in the parties and their policies will be restored.

A hue and cry was made about the Vohra report regarding the nexus between politicians and criminals. Instead of taking corrective action, the rulling party and the opposition parties remained content by trading charges against each other about the criminalisation of politics. The rhetoric of the parties on this issue appeared to display their keenness to discredit each other before the people rather than their sincere desire to root out this evil.

Another alarming tendency in politics in recent times is the parties' deriving satisfaction at their opponents' misfortunes rather than their own achievements. An example of this kind is the claim of the Congress party that its members were in an upbeat mood as the BJP was faced with a problem of dissensions in Gujarat, Maharashtra and Rajasthan. Similarly the BJP and the other opposition parties derived immense satisfaction with the Congress party's discomfiture when some of its dissidents raised a banner of revolt. These reactions point to a negative attitude on their part. Instead of their feeling happy about the weakening of another party, they should concentrate on strengthening their own party and propagating their policies.

The Prime Minister promised that a Temple as well as a Masjid would be constructed at Ayodhya. But so far neither has been built. His Govt. promised that the investigation of Rajiv Gandhi assassination case would be completed by the end of 1995. But the report of the Jain Commission was no where near completion by that time. He had succeeded in his tactics by keeping silent on some issues and by pacifying the people with a stop gap promise for the time being. The Government's reference to the Supreme Court to state whether a temple existed at the site of the Babri Masjid is a classic example in this respect.

The opposition parties could not enhance their own reputation, either. Instead of picking up the specific failures or deficiencies of the Government, they frittered away their energies in staging walk-outs, obstructing the proceedings in Parliament by rushing to the well of the Houses and shouting slogans and forcing the presiding officers to adjourn the Houses. This situation reached its climax in the winter session of 1995 when both the Houses of the Parliament were forced to adjourn on 12 consecutive working days without transacting any business except for a few things like the ratification of the extension of president's rule in Jammu and Kashmir.

Even if their concern to get at the bottom of the Telecom contracts issue was genuine, they cannot justify their obstructionist attitude in the Parliament. They would not have lost anything by allowing a debate on the issue. Their respect for the Parliament should have been shown by going through the agenda set for the session. Parliament is expected to set an example to others in maintaining decency and decorum. Therefore, every member of Parliament owes a duty to the public to keep up the dignity of the House to which he/she belongs irrespective of his/her party affiliation.

Either by nature or due to exigencies of the situation, the Prime Minister gave an impression of allowing things to take their own course instead of trying to shape the events to suit the requirements. This has encouraged some people to create a few piquant situations.

The Election Commission was asserting itself at times causing embarrassment to the Government by making some statements needlessly using strong words. Commenting on some of the recent judgements, Nani Palkivala and a few others have expressed that the Supreme Court was acting like an extended arm of the Executive. Karnataka and Tamilnadu are locked up in a stalemate with regard to the sharing of the Cauvery waters. Although the crops are said to be drying, the central Government has not done anything to find a solution lest it should hurt the feelings of the people of one state or the other.

The general feeling is that a Laissez-faire management was being resorted to by the Government. Even though non-interference in the functioning of institutions is considered a virtue, the Government should not fail to project its image of strength, prestige and a preeminent position in order to ensure that the institutions and the different constituents of democracy would not overstep their powers and the established conventions.

3

Dissidence in Political Parties

The composition of the political parties and their working have a direct bearing on the functioning of the democracy in our country. Therefore, the people are much concerned about the ever-increasing dissidence within the parties, the way it is being tackled, the persons changing their parties often and the formation of too many parties.

In any political party, differences are bound to occur in the views of its leaders on any particular issue or a policy matter. Naturally, the views of the majority or those of the leadership should prevail in such cases. Those who find themselves in a minority should normally take such things in their stride.

Dissidence is not something new in political parties. Even during the time of Gandhiji and Nehru, dissidence existed in a fairly large measure. But there used to be considerable restraint in dealing with the dissidents.

In recent times, the dissidence in political parties has increased to a phenomenal level. With the changing times, the quality and purpose of dissidence also have undergone a sea change. In good old days, the dissidents used to remain content by voicing their dissent on any issue. But, of late, the dissidents are often crossing the limits of the party discipline. They are going all out to embarrass the leadership by their utterances and actions. They also ensure that they are widely publicised in the media.

The leadership also is often adopting an attitude of intolerance of any dissent. It is a pity that many times the differences between the supporters of the leadership and the dissidents have led to verbal clashes as well as physical scuffles. The dissidents can be classified into four categories, generally. Those who become dissidents because of their personal animosity for the leadership belong to the first category. Perhaps, the examples of Arjun Singh's exit from the Congress (I) and of Chandra Shekhar's parting of ways from the Janata Dal fall into this category.

The second category consists of those who turn to dissidence when they fail to get positions of power in the party or the party's Government or when they are denied tickets to contest an election to the State Assembly or Parliament. The most recent examples of this category are the Janata Dal, M.L.A.'s led by Manjunath in Karnataka and the Congress M.L.A.'s led by Rajinder Kaur Bhattal in Punjab. The exit of Natwar Singh from the Congress before the Lok Sabha elections in 1996 also falls into this category.

The people who would put the blame on the leadership for an election debacle fall into the third category. They would either demand a change of leadership or would leave the party to seek greener pastures elsewhere. S.D. Samasundaram, Kannappan and C. Aranganayagam of the AIADMK, Rajesh Pilot, K. Karunakaran and Balram Jakhar in the Congress can be classified in this category.

These people should have the guts to share the blame for the poor results of their parties in the election. For, they would surely have shared the credit if their parties had emerged victorious and enjoyed the fruits of power.

The fourth category consists of the people who differ with the leadership on a policy matter or the reaction of the party to an issue or an event. G.K. Moopanar, P. Chidambaram and M. Arunachalam left the Congress when they did not like the party forging an electoral tie-up with the AIADMK.

But all the dissidents need not necessarily leave a party.

Also, the dissidents should not be looked upon as rebels. In fact, there are instances of the one-time dissidents having taken control of the parties some time later, with the majority swinging in their favour.

The trend in the recent times indicates that the leaders are trying to settle their personal scores at the earliest opportunity taking advantage of their relative strengths in the party at any given time. A tinge of authoritarianism and arbitrariness is evident in some of the disciplinary actions taken by a few parties after the recent Lok Sabha elections in 1996.

The Janta Dal expelled Ramakrishna Hegde for his criticism of that party's decision to form a coalition Government at the Centre with the help of several other parties. Maneka Gandhi too was expelled for her remarks against Deve Gowda for the alleged clearance of the Cogentrix thermal power project disregarding the environmental aspects of it.

Narasimha Rao forced a reluctant Digvijay Singh to drop five ministers from the Madhya Pradesh Government for allegedly having worked against the official candidates of the Congress in the Lok Sabha elections in 1996. Digvijay Singh himself has dismissed Akhand Pratap Singh Yadav, Minister for Animal Husbandry for having criticised the Chief Minister.

The B.J.P. had expelled Shankar Sinh Vaghela in a bid to quell the dissidence within the party in Gujarat. The immediate provocation was his angry reaction to the show cause notice issued by the President of the State Unit of the party questioning his intentions to hold a rally in Ahmedabad on the 20th of August in 1996.

In the AIADMK, some erstwhile ministers like C. Arangnayagam, Kannappan and S.D. Somasundaram were expelled from the party for having criticised Jayalalitha and her friend, Sasikala. Indeed, this list will become too long, if the disciplinary actions in the other parties also have to be mentioned here.

If democracy has to flourish in the country, the political parties aspiring to form the Governments at the centre and the states should observe democratic norms within their parties,first. Some of the parties are in the grip of the same individuals for long durations. This is because either elections are not held at regular intervals or they are held as a farce to elect the same persons, repeatedly.

The parties would do well to formulate a code of conduct for themselves. First of all, the dissidents in a party should not ventilate their grievances outside the party forums. Often the press is blamed for giving undue publicity to them to make the news a little sensational. But, the press would not be able to do it, if the concerned party members observe restraint. Many times, they say something in the heat of the moment and retract from their statements by saying that they were misquoted.

The leaders in charge of the parties should also display a greater degree of tolerance for the criticism and the so called acts of indiscipline of their party members. Expulsion from a party should be done only as a last resort after following the various steps like issuing a warning, a charge sheet, a show cause notice etc. in succession, as far as possible.

The deserters of the party as well as those expelled from it should not be admitted into the other parties at least for a period of three months. Norms should be also fixed for recognising a party formed by a dissident group claiming to have split the parent party. For forming new political parties also, some conditions about a minimum number of members etc. should be laid down.

The corruption and criminal cases against many politicians and their close relatives have shattered the image of the political parties, already. In their bid to gain power, if the political parties hurl wild charges of acts of omission and commission, against one another, ultimately all of them will become the laughing stock of the people.

It is high time that the politicians did some introspection and put their houses in order. Even if they cannot set an example of good conduct and service to the Nation, they should not atleast become symbols of corruption, criminalisation of politics and fall in moral standards.

4

Multi Member Election Commission-Some Flaws to be Set Right

T.N. Seshan has demonstrated how vulnerable the politicians are to the threat of disqualification for election to Parliament and the State Legislatures. By and large, he succeeded in limiting the candidates' election expenses and in keeping the walls in the towns and villages clean. He deserves all the acclaim he received for this.

But, his stand on the issue of photo identity cards to all the voters does not appear to be practicable. Apart from the huge expenditure involved, it is not easy for the illiterate masses in the villages and the slums of the towns to preserve their identity cards carefully. Added to this, the numerous mistakes in the cards issued would have made confusion worse confounded. No doubt, an attempt should be made to issue identity cards. But the stipulation that one cannot vote without an identity card is unreasonable. The Bombay High Court has rightly stepped in to solve this tangle.

The politicians once again seemed to have proved their skill at their games. They all (barring a few exceptions like Laloo Prasad Yadav) appeared to have endorsed his writ on the issue of photo-identity cards. But the scheme is scuttled because of their lack of sincerity. Their calculation that time will solve the problem has proved to be correct.

Ever since he took over as the Chief Election Commissioner,

he had been in the headlines of the newspapers and the electronic media very often for his actions either because of their controversial nature or his style of functioning.

The appointment of M.S. Gill and G.V.G. Krishnamurthy as Election Commissioners with equal status and powers of the CEC had set him on the war path. He succeeded in keeping the Election Commissioners out of action, for nearly 21 months, with the aid of the interim order of the Supreme Court in November 1993, upholding his plea that the Election Commissioners cannot be equal to the CEC. A lot of dirty line was washed in public by all three of them hurling accusations on one another.

The power of the print media had given a boost to his image as a no-nonsense and uncompromising constitutional authority, keen on cleansing the electoral process in the country. No doubt, his intentions appear to be good. But it is wrong to assume that the elections held so far have been faulty or would have been affected by the impersonations, rigging and money power.

It is doubtless that these evils are most abominable and have to be eliminated. However, the results of the elections would not have been affected by these malpractices more than marginally. The fact that even great and powerful leaders have lost their elections and several ruling parties were ousted from power by the people through the ballot box is a testimony in this regard.

The Supreme Court has done well by directing D.S. Bagga, the Deputy Election Commissioner to hand over the charge of the Election Commission to M.S. Gill in 1995 during the absence of T.N. Seshan. The impropriety of T.N. Seshan's action in delegating his powers to D.S. Bagga before leaving for the U.S. on a month-long vacation on June 29 is too glaring and has rightly come in for severe criticism. Obviously, T.N. Seshan had overstepped the limits of his powers in his anxiety to keep the two Election Commissioners out of the picture. Perhaps, he would not have lost anything by asking one of the two Election Commissioners to be in charge of the Election

Commission until his return from the U.S.

But, it is surprising that the Government has not done anything to correct the situation. The reason for this could be its anxiety to avoid a controversy. For, in all probability, T.N. Seshan as well as a few political parties and individuals would have accused the Government of interference in the working of the Election Commission. But, it is to be examined whether it is proper for the Government to abstain from its duty even if it is for avoiding a controversy. At least now, the Government should specify the rules as to who should be in-charge of the Election Commission when a Chief Election Commissioner goes on leave in a multi member Election Commission as well as a single member Election Commission. It should not expect the Supreme Court to deal with such situations, every time.

(So far, Seshan's reaction to the Supreme Court's verdict is not known to the public. Some people are predicting that he might resign from the office of CEC. But those who know his fighting qualities would not rule out his continuance in the post.)

Despite the well-meaning advice of the Supreme Court to the ECs to "forget and forgive" and to "start on a clean slate of mutual respect and confidence" it is extremely doubtful whether the CEC and ECs could "eschew their egos and work in a spirit of camaradarie". The many controversies and quarrels between T.N. Seshan and other election commissioners indicate the lack of cohesion in the working of the Election Commission. The latest example (in December 1997) is the quarrel between M.S. Gill and G.V.G. Krishnamurthy on the issue of elections in Shiv Sena.

With the same status and powers, the CEC and the two EC's form a "troika" heading the Election Commission jointly. The condition that the decision of the majority would prevail in case of a difference of opinion would make it difficult to achieve harmony in the Commission's work. It appears that there is little scope for them to work individually. They may have to sit together in a room almost every day to decide on the day to day matters like appointments, retrenchments, transfers, disciplinary actions, allocation of work etc. The staff would not know to whom they have to report and from whom they have to receive instructions. There is a possibility of every one of them being embarrassed sometime or other when he finds himself in a minority on any of the above issues and the same comes to light. They may also have to visit any place together to take spot decisions.

Taking decisions on dates for holding elections, arrangements for maintenance of law and order and disposal of election petitions could become cumbersome and difficult. Therefore, for ensuring smooth working in the Election Commission, it should be clearly mentioned on what kind of matters the decisions should be taken collectively. In the day to day administrative work, either the CEC should be given full powers or a clearcut allocation of duties should be made.

To say that the CEC is like a chairman chosen to merely preside over a meeting seems to be an over simplification. In the "bodies" like CBDT, CBCE, Law Commission and Planning Commission, the Chairman (Vice-Chairman in the case of Planning Commission), is not merely meant to preside over the meetings. He/She is given over riding powers over the other members. Moreover, the members are assigned specific duties.

G.V.G. Krishnamurthy cited the analogy of the High Court and Supreme Court Chief Justices and the Judges to drive home the point that in taking decisions (giving judgements) the Chief Justices are like the other judges and some times they could find themselves in a minority. But this example may not be applicable to the working of the Election Commission. In courts, the majority decisions prevail in disposal of the cases only. A Chief Justice exercises his own discretionary powers in the day to day administrative work, recommendation for appointment of Judges and taking disciplinary action on erring judicial officers etc.

Therefore, for smooth working of the Election Commission, the duties of the CEC and ECs should be spelt out broadly. The matters on which it is obligatory on the part of CEC and ECs to arrive at decisions collectively either unanimously or by a majority should also be clearly mentioned.

5

Glaring Anomalies in Poll Pacts

(The situation in U.P. as it prevailed on the eve of the elections to the State Assembly in October 1996 is presented here to highlight the anomalies in poll pacts in general.)

The main contenders for power in the U.P. Assembly elections were the U.F. -BKKP combine, the BSP-Congress alliance and the BJP-Samata Party team.The contest between them was expected to be quite tough. A noteworthy point was that in U.P. the Congress and the Janata Dal were reduced to the uneviable position of playing second fiddle to the BSP and the SP respectively.

The BSP was contesting 300 seats, leaving the remaining 125 seats to the Congress. These parties had projected Mayawati as their choice for the post of the Chief Minister. Although, Rajesh Pilot and a few other leaders of the Congress criticised the poll pact, a vast majority of the party was reconciled to it, having taken into consideration the ground realities of the party's strength.

By naming Mulayam Singh Yadav to lead the poll campaign of the U.F., Deve Gowda had displayed his political skill in handling his party's poll partners. The SP, which had been entrusted with the responsibility of allocating the seats to the constituents of the U.F. and B.K.K.P. had taken a lion's share of 265 seats for itself. The Janata Dal and the Left parties were given around 50 and 25 seats respectively. The All India Indira

Congress (T) got about 30 seats.

Ajit Singh, who seems to be always on the move to be on the right side of the power had left the Congress a few days earlier and joined the Bharatiya Kisan Kamgar Party (BKKP) of Mahendra Singh Tikhait as its President. Mulayam Singh Yadav appeared to be quite generous in allotting as many as 40 seats to this new found ally of the U.F.

The BJP allotted nine seats to the Samata Party and retained for itself the remaining four hundred sixteen seats. The BJP and the UF had refrained from projecting their candidates for the Chief Ministership, although it was almost certain that Kalyan Singh and Mulayam Singh Yadav were most likely to be chosen by their respective parties.

There were many glaring anomalies in these poll pacts. For instance, the BSP was an electoral ally of the National Conference in Jammu and Kashmir, whereas the Congress was fighting the elections against the National Conference. In the Lok Sabha elections held in May 1996 too, the BSP was aligned with the Shiromani Akali Dal which was the main opponent of the Congress in Punjab. The Congress was supporting the U.F. Government at the Centre and fighting the elections in U.P. against the U.F.

Similarly, it was strange that N.D. Tiwari who was demanding the withdrawal of support of the Congress to the then Mulayam Singh Yadav Government in U.P., had forged an alliance of his party with the U.F. whose dominant partner in that election was the Samajwadi Party.

The alliance between the BJP and the Samata Party had come to stay ever since the Assembly elections in Bihar in 1994. George Fernandes, who was once a bitter critic of the BJP has now become its staunch supporter. But, the people have learnt to take such anomalies and political turn-arounds in their stride.

When the SP and BSP fought the elections as poll partners in the 1993 U.P. Assembly elections they could get only a very slender majority over the BJP's tally of 175. They fell far short of an absolute majority and could form a coalition Government only with the support of the Congress and the Janata Dal. When they fought the recent Lok Sabha elections separately, the SP and BSP could win only 17 and 8 seats respectively as agianst the BJP's handsome tally of 54 out of the 85 Lok Sabha seats from U.P.

But the leaders whose personal egos get the better of their parties' avowed policies would not learn their lessons from the statistics of such election results. If secularism is such an important policy for them and if their fears of the BJP considered by them to be communal are genuine, these parties should have sunk their differences and put up a joint front against the BJP.

The reasons for not doing so are quite simple. Every party puts its own interests above anything else. Most of the leaders are interested in attaining positions of power and ensuring their own importance. The differences between Mulayam Singh Yadav and Kanshi Ram are so wide that their parties are considered to be bitter enemies of each other.

If the BJP had won an absolute majority, it would have tried to interprete it as the people's verdict against the U.F. Government at the Centre. Similarly, if the BJP failed to give a good account of itself, all the other parties would have called it a victory for the secular forces.

The importance that the U.F. was attaching to that election was evident from the number of visits that Deve Gowda had paid to that State over the three months prior to the elections. He made so many announcements about the development schemes in that State that the Election Commissioner, G.V.G. Krishna Moorthy felt it necessary to caution the P.M.

Although, a facade of unity was being maintained, serious differences were simmering between the parties as also between the leaders of the U.F. While the transfer of Romesh Bhandari to U.P. as its Governor was frowned upon by the "left parties", the S.P. had not taken kindly to the appointment of T.S.R. Subramanian as the Cabinet Secretary.

The announcement about the Government's intention to form Uttarakhand State by dividing U.P. had come in for severe criticism from several quarters, particularly from the C.P.M.

The meeting of Deve Gowda with Bal Thackeray had sent the wrong signals to his party leaders like V.P. Singh as well as to the Left parties and the Congress. Its adverse effect was not yet nullified totally, in spite of his repeated assertions that the meeting had no political significance.

His frequent meetings with P.V. Narasimha Rao had drawn the ire of the Communist parties. But, he could not avoid those meetings as his Government depended on the support of the Congress party. The Cauvery waters dispute and the Almatti dam issue were threatening to snowball into major problems very soon. The Telugu Desam Party which is a partner of the U.F. had already embarked on a war path. As his home State, Karnataka was a party to these disputes, the Prime Minister's task had become all the more difficult in finding solutions for them.

The woes of the Congress were not less than those of the U.F. The image of the Congress had been tarnished by several charges of corruption levelled against some top leaders of the party. The dissidents were demanding the resignation of P.V. Narasimha Rao from the post of the President of the Party. The results of that election were expected to have a far reaching effect on the leadership issue in the party.

The earlier happenings in Gujarat had disproved the common belief that the BJP is a cadre based and a disciplined party. People started to believe that it is as vulnerable to groupism and internal revolts as any other party in our country. The hawala cases against some of its leaders had sullied the image of that party.

The threat of the "Red brigade", "Blue brigade" and "Chunav Sena" of the SP, the BSP and the BJP swarming the scene, creating large scale law and order problems loomed large on the horizon. The Government and the Election Commission were well advised to take all preventive steps and ensure the deployment of sufficient police personnel for peaceful conduct of the polls.

Finally, one had to give a thought to the post-election scenario that was likely to emerge. If one of the parties, namely, the BJP, the SP and the BSP failed to secure an absolute majority by itself, the conditions of instability of the Government would not be eliminated.

Therefore, the Government and the political parties should sit together and come out with the necessary poll reforms or constitutional amendments to ensure stability of a Government for a fixed tenure and to avoid mid-term polls and by-elections which are causing avoidable expenditure to the exchequer and at times creating serious law and order problems.

6

Suggestions to Check Unhealthy Trends in Elections

This chapter consists of an article written by this author before the general elections held in May 1996 to depict the electoral scene prevailing at that time.

Ever since the schedule for the elections to the Lok Sabha and six state Assemblies was announced, there has been a hectic flurry of political activity.

The selection of the candidates by the various parties has left a bitter trail of dissatisfaction and disappointment among large sections of their members. Most of the sitting members and quite a few close relatives of some influencial leaders were given the tickets in preference to other aspirants who claimed to be more deserving.

A few of the leaders who were denied tickets to contest the elections for one reason or the other have crossed over to other parties. Yet others formed their own parties overnight. Some of them are contesting as independent candidates also.

If the selection of the candidates was done a few months before the announcement of the elections, the position would not have become so confusing on the eve of the elections. Because of this confusion, the voters would find it difficult to make up their minds as to whom they should vote for.

Electoral alliances have been forged hastily between some

parties. The only aim of such alliances seems to be either to improve their chances of winning a few more seats or to ensure the defeat of some party which they do not like. The J.D. and S.P. which were hostile to each other till recently have come together in U.P. The B.J.P. and Samata party entered into an alliance in Bihar in spite of their ideological differences.

The Congress has finally joined hands with the AIADMK after being indecisive for quite a long time in choosing between the D.M.K. and the AIADMK. The D.M.K. which is criticising the Congress now would have been probably singing its praises if the latter chose to align with the D.M.K.

The B.S.P. has entered into an alliance with the Shiromani Akali Dal which is opposed to the Congress in Punjab. Yet, Kanshiram says that the B.S.P. is keeping its options open to support either the Congress or the B.J.P. according to the situation in the post-election scenario. Perhaps, the B.S.P. would not mind supporting even the N.F.-L.F. combine also, if it could patch up with Mulayam Singh Yadav whom it hates at present.

People are naturally at a loss to understand as to how these alliances are being forged without any common programme or ideology or a commitment to continue with the alliance for a reasonably long period. Obviously, expediency and opportunism seem to have influenced the parties in forging the electoral alliances rather than principles and policies or the interests of the people.

If a party 'A' fights an election in alliance with 'B' against 'C' and after the election it withdraws from the alliance and joins hands with 'C', it amounts to nothing short of playing a political fraud on the people. But, unfortunately such things have happened and are likely to happen in future also.

Although, almost all the parties have been talking about giving larger representation to women, none of them has proved its sincerity in this regard. Very few women have been given tickets to contest the elections. Even if 30% of the tickets are given to women, there is no guarantee that 30% of the elected members are going to be women. Therefore, the best way of ensuring sufficient representation to women is to elect one man and one woman from every constituency. If the total number of seats has to be kept at the present level, fresh demarcation of the present constituencies may be done by merging roughly two of them into one.

The manifestoes of the parties seem to be full of empty promises. Many of them are being repeated before every election. If they are released at least six months before an election, the people will have time to study them and to seek clarifications. The manifestoes should contain details of their achievements also in addition to the promises.

The Janata Party says that it will abolish the personal income tax if it comes to power. Considering the bleak chances of that party coming to power, this promise does not seem to be of any value at all.

The J.D. harps on social justice and reservation of jobs in private sector. When it was in power at the centre, it has done pretty little in implementing these programmes.

The C.P.M. promises to supply drinking water to every village. One would naturally wonder as to why it could not fulfil this promise at least in West Bengal where it has been in power for nearly two decades continuously.

The Congress keeps on postponing the dates for the fulfilment of its promises like the abolition of child labour, providing compulsory primary education, poverty alleviation etc. by five years or so on the eve of every general election.

The plight of the poor and the lower middle class people has not improved much during its long rule of more than four decades. They are groaning under acute conditions of unemployment, rising prices, dearth of housing and exploitation.

The B.J.P. says that it will remove the article 370 pertaining to the special status of Jammu & Kashmir from the constitution. It is also advocating acquisition of nuclear weapons for countering the threat from Pakistan. Both these proposals are fraught with far reaching ramifications. The promise to eliminate corruption does not carry conviction after the recent revelations of the hawala scandal. Evidently, being unable to conceive any other programme to enthuse the people, it has once again revived its programme to build a Ram Temple at Ayodhya.

The All India Indira Congress (Tiwari) promises to undo much of whatever the Narasimha Rao Government has done with regard to the liberalisation of the economic policy. It also promises to expedite the investigation into the Rajiv Gandhi assissination case.

The regional parties are promising to solve the local problems. Some of them are trying to cash in on the image of NTR and MGR. The D.M.K. and Tamil Maanila Congress are hoping to exploit the popularity of the cine actor, Rajnikant among his fans, to their advantage.

The Supreme Court has ruled that the expenses incurred by a party should also be treated as a part of the election expenses of its candidates. Suppose, a Central leader visits the constituency of a candidate in a helicopter, should the expenses be treated as having been incurred by the candidate? The Central leader might not visit all the other constituencies. In such a case, why should the candidates from the other constituencies be asked to accept a proportionate part of it to be added to their election expenditure? Understandably, the Election Commission has expressed its difficulty in enforcing this rule. If only such ruling was given a few months before the announcement of elections, the parties concerned could have understood its implications and proper norms would have been formulated for the political parties to follow.

The Election Commission has recommended the enhancement of the limit on poll expenditure to a whopping Rs. 15 lakhs and Rs. 6 lakhs for each candidate of Lok Sabha and Assembly election respectively from the existing limits of Rs. 4.5 lakhs and Rs. 1.5 lakhs. The Government is reluctant to accept this recommendation. Interestingly, Kanshiram has suggested reduction of the limit of election expenses to Rs. 1 lakh per candidate. (The recommendation of the E.C. to enhance the poll expenses has been accepted by the

Government on the eve of the 1998 Lok Sabha elections).

The E.C. is likely to receive a lot of election petitions with charges against the winning candidates about having exceeded the limits on election expenditure. All these points should have been discussed and finalised well before the announcement of the election dates instead of trying to solve a problem after allowing it to crop up.

The E.C. is passing orders imposing restrictions on the Government in dealing with even matters which do not appear to have any effect on the voters' minds to influence their voting pattern. Some of the examples in this respect are the embargo on the export of cotton bales and on filling the post of the Executive Director of UTI.

Instead of being over enthusiastic in such matters, the EC could have put restrictions on the formation of new parties and on changing of the parties by their members at least between the dates of announcement of elections and declaration of the election results.

As usual, there are many predictions about the number of seats, each party is likely to win. Most of the pre-poll surveys indicate the likelihood of a hung parliament coming into being. Of course, such poll surveys are often proving to be wrong, as it happened in 1977 and 1980 in India, in 1992 in England and less than a month ago in South Korea.

But still, the possibility of a hung parliament coming into existence deserves to be studied and a solution worked out before-hand to avert a constitutional impasse. In order to avoid horse trading and formation of absurd alliances for establishing an artificial majority, the parties should have agreed in principle that the party or the coalition of parties (formed well before the elections) emerging as the single largest party should have the right to form the next Government and such a Government will not be removed from office for a minimum period of three years.

Another point of serious concern to the people is the tendency of some leaders to contest from two constituencies.

In case, they are elected from both the constituencies, a by election would be necessitated in one of the constituencies as the elected person cannot represent more than one constituency. A by election would cost a lot of money and would also at times create serious law and order problems. Therefore, such a practice should be stopped forthwith.

In case a member of an assembly or the Rajya Sabha wants to contest an election to the Lok Sabha, he should be made to pay Rs. 1.5 lakhs or so for causing a by election. Moreover, he/ she should be required to resign first before contesting the election.

The situation and problems highlighted in this chapter hold good in respect of many elections that have taken place since 1996. Perhaps they will remain so with regard to future elections also, unless suitable corrective steps are taken.

7

Perks and Emoluments of Legislators

Now (in 1997) there is a clamour from the legislators for an increase in their salaries and improving their pension benefits. It is indeed amusing to read the reported statements of some of the MPs in this regard. While one has stated that they are 'starving', another has stated that their fate is worse than that of "bonded labourers" and yet another said that they have "become the laughing stock of the nation" because they are earning a mere Rs. 50 per day which is only slightly more than the minimum wage of Rs. 46 per day being paid to mazdoors.

India is indeed a country of paradoxes. It is really a wonder as to how the inflation rate is reported to be contained within four per cent, even after the recent hike in the prices of the petroleum products. The common man is surprised as to how the prices of his daily needs are rising continuously despite the government's claim of quite a low rate of inflation.

The news that the Karnataka Assembly "adopted without any discussion two Bills aimed at doubling the allowances of ministers and legislators" is quite interesting. It is reported that this will entail an annual expenditure of Rs. 7 crore to the State Government. The Law Minister, M.C. Nanaiah, stated that the increase became necessary due to `inflation'!.

Salaries and Perks

There seems to be a rare unanimity among the members

of almost all the parties in Parliament and the state legislatures, when they deal with any Bill to increase their own salaries and perks.

In 1967, when the DMK came to power in Tamil Nadu, the then chief minister, C.N. Annadurai, announced that the ministers in his government would reduce their salaries by a half. Later, in 1991 Jayalalitha who became the chief minister said that she would draw a salary of Re 1 only per month. There are a few others also, like Pupul Jayakar who claimed to have worked on a salary of Re 1 only, while holding their prestigeous and sometimes powerful positions. But all of them appear to be mere gimmicks only when it is realised that the perks and allowances of the posts they held are far higher than the salaries they have foregone. Indeed, the government could afford to give their salaries in full. If any people are so keen on giving away a part of their salaries, perhaps they could donate the same to some charitable organisations.

Very recently, the retirement benefits of the vice-president of India have been hiked substantially. A little later, the perks of the members of the Parliament like the constituency allowance, telephone allowance etc. were also almost doubled.

Pension Benefits

Ram Vilas Paswan says that every MP should receive a pension regardless of the duration of his membership of the House. If this is justified, why can't the employees in the government, the PSUs and the private companies also be eligible for such a rule?

Jayanti Natarajan says that the parliamentarians must be better paid and looked after if they are expected to remain incorruptible. But it is generally an accepted fact that corruption is not necessarily the result of poverty or low salaries. Essentially, it is the result of greed and an impulse to exploit the needy and to misuse one's power and influence to one's own advantage. Therefore, many people believe that the richer and privileged people are far more corrupt in their official and business dealings.

If any Indian legislator compares his/her salary with that of a British MP or an American Senator, he/she should be advised to ponder over the difference in the per capita income of the peoples they represent.

It is not known how much of the Rs. 1 crore per year given to each MP for developmental projects in his/her constituency is being properly used for the purpose it is meant. It is the general opinion of the people that their representatives in the legislatures are living in luxury.

If they are so dissatisfied with their lot, the people wonder as to why they should stand for election, often spending lakhs of rupees from their own pockets or from their party funds. Surely, there is no dearth of people to take their place. They are ready to accept the existing salaries and perks and also to work more vigorously and sincerely for the betterment of the country.

Indeed, their clamour for their own benefits leaving the millions of the people they represent in stark poverty is glaringly in contrast to the noble spirit of self denial expressed in the words "thy need is greater than mine."

Starving Legislators

Many of the starving legislators are said to have amassed a lot of wealth for themselves and their relatives. Perhaps, only a small percentage of them is remaining in more or less the same financial condition as at the beginning of their tenures as legislators. In fact, there is a popular demand that it should be made compulsory for every legislator to declare his/her assets at the time of taking oath as a member of a House and again within a fortnight of his/her having ceased to be a legislator. If the government is serious in curbing corruption, it should implement this measure to start with, in order to set an example to others to follow.

The implementation of the recommendations of the Fifth Pay Commission as agreed to by the government after the negotiations with the unions of the Central Government employees in certain categories would cast an additional burden of around Rs. 18,350 crore on the exchequer in the current financial year (1997-98). The government has accepted the main demand of the unions to add 40 per cent DA to the basic pay instead of the 20 per cent offered by the government earlier.

The government appeared to be so anxious to avoid the threatened strike by its employees from September 24 of 1997 that it gave the impression that it would have agreed to even a higher percentage if the unions so demanded. We can expect that very soon, the employees of the PSUs will demand a hike in thier salaries too. Naturally, that will be followed by an increase in the salaries of the employees in the private companies.

Abnormal Increase

This is bound to result in an abnormal increase in the prices of almost all the commodities. May be, the business class, rich landlords and the salaried class in the high income bracket will not be much affected by such an increase in the prices. But the salaried class in the low income group, the unemployed/under employed people, the rural folk engaged in seasonal agricultural work and those from the unorganised sector are going to suffer very badly in due course.

Therefore, it is high time that the government took a comprehensive view of the whole economy and took such measures that would benefit all sections of the people equitably. This is very essential to prevent the disparities between them getting further widened. May be, a formula can be worked out to revise the salaries of the employees and also the legislators once in five years or so on the basis of the increase in the per capita income of the people in general.

The legislators should not appear to misuse their power to increase their own salaries and perks from time to time without first ensuring the improvement of the condition of the poor people they represent. They should have a fear of being accused of putting "self before service."

8

Common Man's View Points on a Few Topics

The common man constitutes the back-bone of a society. The success of a system is usually measured by the amount of satisfaction it gives the common man. But, strangely enough, the voice of the common man is rarely heard by the leaders.

The common man expects the rules to be simple and rational. He is often upset with many unreasonable things happening in the country, but he feels helpless to set them right. The common man's view points on a few of such things are furnished below:

(1) It was reported that Nitish Kumar of the Samata Party has resigned from the Bihar Legislative Assembly within a few days after being elected as a member of the House. Earlier, V.P. Singh resigned from the Lok Sabha. Like this, M. Karunanidhi resigned from the Tamilnadu Assembly in 1991. N.T. Rama Rao was elected from two constituencies in the elections to the Andhra Pradesh State Legislative Assembly. After the results were announced, he vacated his seat from the Tekkali Constituency. Prasanna Kumar Patsani, a sitting member of the Orissa Legislative Assembly was pitted against J.B. Patnaik in the by-election held in Begunia constituency in Orissa. If he had won, he would have been required to vacate one of the two seats. These are only a few examples of this kind.

Such resignations are being resorted to by the members of many parties as well as independents in most of the states and at the centre. Whatever be the reasons for such resignations, they are resulting in a heavy expenditure on the exchequer for holding by-elections to fill up those vacancies. By elections are also causing avoidable tension and some times serious law and order problems.

One wonders as to why these people should have stood for the elections at all, if they were not serious about remaining as the members of those Houses to represent the constituencies from where they were elected. Some others keep on flitting from a State Assembly/council to the Lok Sabha/Rajya Sabha or vice versa, thus creating vacancies in those Houses.

In order to discourage this unhealthy trend, it should be stipulated that an elected member of a house will have to pay Rs. 1 lakh or so if he resigns from a state Assembly/Council and Rs. 2 lakhs or so if he resigns from the Lok Sabha/Rajya Sabha. It should be further stipulated that he should not be eligible to stand for an election to the State Assembly/Council and Lok Sabha/Rajya Sabha for a period of two years from the date, his resignation takes effect.

(2) The recent election to the Bihar Assembly (in 1995) was conducted after several postponements. Thus, the election process could not be completed by 15/3/95 when the 5 year term of the then Legislative Assembly ended. Theoretically, the term of the Laloo Prasad Yadav Ministry ended by then. However, good sense prevailed with the Central Government and the Laloo Prasad Yadav Government was allowed to continue. But unfortunately, all the results of the election did not seem likely to be declared by the end of March 95. Therefore, the Union Government imposed President's rule on the 26th of March to enable the Parliament to pass a vote on account for the State before 31/3/95. This has resulted in accusations of the Congress Government and the Election Commission by the Janata Dal. Laloo Prasad Yadav said that the Chief Election Commissioner was partisan and acting in an arbitrary manner.

Of course, later, to the pleasant surprise of the J.D., it had scored an impressive victory. Laloo Prasad Yadav was installed again as the Chief Minister on the 3rd of April 95. After his party's victory, Laloo Prasad Yadav showered praise on T.N. Seshan for the way in which he conducted the election!

Many people wondered whether there was no way out for avoiding the imposition of the President's rule just for 8 days. Surely, it should be possible to make necessary amendments to the rules/constitution to allow the incumbent Government to continue even after its term is over, under extra ordinary and unforeseen circumstances. For taking a vote on account, the outgoing Assembly could be convened for one or two days, if it was absolutely necessary and if no substitute procedure could be formulated.

Imposition of President's rule gives rise to suspicion about the motives of the central Government and also ruffles passions of the political parties.

(3) Whenever a popular leader passes away, naturally the people mourn his death. The Government also is justified in paying its tribute in a fitting manner. But people are usually disgusted at the undue fuss that is made on such occasions. Declaration of too many holidays, observing state mourning for a long duration and squandering money and time in V.I.P.'s visits from far and wide for attending the funeral are often turning the people's sympathy and respect to the departed soul into revulsion and disapprobation of the Government for causing needless hardship to them and avoidable expense to the Exchequer.

Government should formulate standard rules to be followed on such occasions. Government offices should not be closed for more than one day. If they are closed for more than one day in exceptional cases, essential services should be allowed to function after the first day in all the Government and Public Sector offices. Radio and T.V. should be allowed to go on with their normal programmes except for one hour in a day during the period of state mourning for paying tributes or recitation of scriptures from holy books. The state mourning too should not be for more than 3 days except for "serving President and Prime Minister." V.I.P's within the town or nearby towns/ villages only should attend such funerals. They should avoid visits from far off places at the expense of the Government. A tribute can be paid from wherever they happen to be. The National Flag can be flown at half mast during the entire period of the state mourning as per the norms. Indeed, there are many ways of perpetuating the memory of a departed leader other than by spending lots of money in the funeral in the aforesaid manner.

(4) It is reported that some Chief Ministes/ Ministes are in the habit of calling officials to their residences at odd hours for holding discussions. People do not have a high opinion about the bureaucrats. They think that the officials are not much concerned about their problems. They also think that many of these officials are arrogant and unresponsive.

In spite of this, people feel that it is not proper for the Chief Ministers/ Ministers to call the officials to their residences at any odd time. Such meetings at the residences of Chief Ministers/ Ministers should be held only in rare cases like an emergency situation or the Chief Minister/ Minister being indisposed.

The Governments are run by the representatives of the people. The representatives should keep in touch with the people by whom they are elected. If they do not listen to the voice of the people and take note of their feelings, they will run the risk of losing the confidence of the people.

9

A Third Alternative to Ensure Stable Governments

Some persons like R. Venkataraman, Vasant Sathe and Pratap Singh Rane have been advocating the adoption of Presidential form of Government in our country.

They feel that if it is done, some of the problems with regard to the present form of Government could be overcome. In the Presidential form of Government, the President is required to be elected by the people directly.

Both these forms of Government have their merits as well as drawbacks. Much depends on the persons occupying the positions of power and the conventions established for ensuring the satisfactory functioning of either of the above forms of Government. If a Prime Minister who has to depend on a majority in the Lok Sabha for the survival of his/her Government could at times become too powerful, an ambitious and power-hungry person elected as a President directly by the people could really play havoc by wielding dictatorial powers.

Therefore, let us examine as to what are the defects in the present form of Government and find out whether it is possible to rectify them by making changes here and there in the rules, electoral procedures and the constitution.

One of the anomalies in the present system is that at times, a party is able to secure an absolute majority in the Lok Sabha/ Vidhan Sabha and form a Government by getting even lower than 35% of the total votes cast in an election. This percentage become still smaller if it is worked out taking the total number of eligible voters into account. But we are thinking that the Governments are representing the will of the majority.

Quite a few candidates are winning elections to Lok Sabha or Vidhan Sabha with very narrow majority of a few hundreds of votes only. For, in a multi-cornered contest, the winning candidate might not have got 50% of the total number of votes polled. An important point lost sight of in all the discussions and debates about electoral reforms is that the will of the people who have voted for the losing candidates is remaining totally ignored and un-represented.

Very often, a lot of horse-trading is done to enlist the support of some parties or some members of Lok Sabha or Vidhan Sabha to form a Government by hook or the crook. Such post-election machinations have led to the formation of Governments by small and opportunistic parties combining together without a common programme or out-look. Single largest party in the Lok Sabha or Vidhan Sabha was forced to sit in opposition many times by such groups of parties.

Defections of the members of Lok Sabha or Vidhan Sabha are often placing a Government's fate in the balance. This is happening in spite of the anti-defection law that is in force, although this law has reduced such defections to some extent.

Many a time, cross voting on important issues has resulted in scuttling Governments' efforts to bring about progressive changes in the society.

The fate of an important leader of any political party seems to be dependent on the result of the election in one constituency from where he/she contests for a seat in the Lok Sabha/Vidhan Sanha. When the party itself acknowledges him/her as its leader it sounds absurd to stipulate that he/she could lead the party in the Lok Sabha/Vidhan Sabha only if he/she can win an election just in one constituency. Often, it is stated that the leader's image is securing votes for his/her party. Another vital question is whether the voters are casting their votes in favour of a party or a candidate of that party.

If a leader loses an election in one constituency, he/she is not gracefully accepting the voters' wishes and waiting till the next General election. There are instances of such leaders installing their dummies as leaders of their legislature parties. Such leaders have got themselves elected in by-elections and replaced the dummy leaders in a short time. Some leaders are contesting from two or more constituencies simultaneously. If a leader gets elected from all the constituencies, he/she retains one seat and resigns from the other seat thus causing a by-election to be held. If he/she is elected from one constituency and is defeated in another constituency, the defeat is simply ignored.

Often, we hear accusations being made against the Prime Minister/Chief Ministers/Ministers about their partiality to their respective constituencies. Is it proper for any of them to give special attention to the development of a tiny constituency from where he/she is elected while he/she is expected to give equal attention to the entire country/State?

Clashes between people of different castes and communities are occurring many times because of the feelings roused by the contesting candidates/parties in a constituency. For winning an election, such candidates are being selected on the basis of their caste or community. In fact, the very basis for demarcating a constituency is arbitrary. Any alteration in the boundaries of a constituency could produce a different result in an election.

Many times, we hear election pandits saying that some parties came to power as a result of the so-called sympathy vote", "negative vote", "anti-establishment vote" etc. If this is so, how could it be ascertained as to when the people have changed their minds?

Filling vacancies caused by the death/resignation of any sitting members of the Lok Sabha or Vidhan Sabha is a cumbersome and costly process. If any candidate of a recognised party dies, the election in the contituency is being countermanded. The chances of some important leader coming to power could be jeopardised because of such an occurrence in his/her constituency.

Dissolution of assemblies is sometimes necessitated prematurely because of a stalemate situation either due to "hung assemblies" coming into being or the Government losing majority in the Lok Sabha/Vidhan Sabha due to floor crossings by some of the ruling party members. In such an event, a fresh election becomes necessary with its attendant problems of law and order and cost.

If a few by-elections are won by the Opposition parties, they are clamouring for the resignation of the Government, interpreting those results as indicative of loss of faith of the people in the Government.

It is difficult to remove all the above mentioned draw-backs of the existing system. However, they can be minimised to a great extent by making a few changes in the procedures, as stated below:

In a General Election, each of the political parties should put up their consolidated lists of candidates contesting the election. For instance, if the number of seats in a Vidhan Sabha is 200, a party can put up the names of candidates not exceeding 200. The party may select the candidates giving representation to women, minorities, backward castes etc. according to its constitutional/policy norms. The party may put up the names of about ten of its important leaders at the top of the list. The names of the rest of the candidates may be included in the list, taking into consideration, their personal popularity, knowledge, capacity, qualifications, geographical representation etc. Suppose, a party wins 55% of the total valid votes cast. Then 55% of the number of the candidates from the top of the list should be declared as elected. In this system, it is considered that the party is given the mandate and not any particular individual. As the names of its important leaders are put at the top, their election becomes almost a certainty.

In the event of no party securing an absolute majority of votes polled, the following procedure could be adopted. Whichever party is the single largest party, it shall have the right to form the Government. There are two ways of making this possible. Let us take a specific example of parties A, B, C and D participating in an election. Let us also assume that their parties have got 35%, 30%, 25% and 10% of the valid votes polled, respectively. As per the above suggestion, the party 'A' should form the Government. In order to make the party attain majority in the Lok Sabha/Vidhan Sabha, such a number of the members of the parties B, C and D should be made to be non-voting members, whereby the ruling party will enjoy a 5% majority in the House. The number of non-voting members in each of these parties should be fixed in the proportion of 30:25:10. They would however have all the other privileges of the members of the Lok Sabha/Vidhan Sabha. If two or more parties want to form an electoral front, the same should be announced at least 6 months in advance of an election. In case they part ways after the election, the lead partner shall enjoy the rights as though it has won the election on its own.

The other way is to stipulate that irrespective of the voting figures in the Lok Sabha/Vidhan Sabha the Government shall have the right to carry on with the normal Government business during its tenure. The voting figures will only be meant for the people to know the stand taken by a party on any issue. This will have its impact on the next election only and not on the stability of the Government of the day. However, for important legislations like constitutional amendments, the Government should be required to have the support of a specified majority of the members.

The reasonableness of this suggestion becomes evident if one takes into account the present pattern of voting on party lines as per the "Whips". When the individual members cannot vote as per their own view on an issue, the result of a division in the Lok Sabha/Vidhan Sabha becomes predetermined.

The tendency for independent candidates to stand for election should be discouraged. If a few independents come together and agree on the order of their names in the list of their candidates, they could be allowed to contest the election.

If a sitting member of a party in the Lok Sabha/Vidhan Sabha dies/resigns or is expelled, the candidate next in the order in the original list of candidates shall automatically fill up that vacancy. Thereby, the expensive and often acrimonious by-elections could be avoided. A party's strength in the Lok Sabha/Vidhan Sabha will remain constant for the tenure for which it is elected.

If any party wins more than 50 per cent of the votes polled, it shall have a right to continue in power for 5 years. But if it forms a Government on the basis of its being the single largest party, its Government shall have a tenure of 3 years only.

As it is assumed that the voters have cast their votes in favour of a party, if any elected member of Lok Sabha/Vidhan Sabha leaves the party, he/she should automatically forfeit his/her seat. The vacancy thus caused shall be filled up as per the procedure already stated.

The power to dismiss a state Government should be removed. The article 356 should be applied in very exceptional circumstances only. When President's rule is imposed, the State Assembly should be kept in an animated suspension. When the President's rule is lifted normally within six months, the Assembly should be allowed to resume functioning.

By adopting this procedure the following specific advantages can be obtained, besides eliminating many of the draw-backs of the existing system.

Every voter feels that his vote has not been cast in vain. All the voters feel that they have been represented by a party for which they have voted. The feeling that their votes have been cast to the defeated candidates would not be there in their minds as is happening now. This is a special feature which is non existent in the elections in countries like the U.K. and the U.S. also.

A situation like a "hung assembly" with no party winning an absolute majority is effectively tackled in this arrangement.

Frequent General Elections due to instability of Governments can be avoided.

A healthy party system will develop very soon for a healthy democracy to flourish.

10

Crisis Facing the BJP Government - Solution for Similar Problems in Future

The people are watching with a bated breath as to what might happen to the BJP Govt. when it seeks a vote of confidence in the Lok Sabha before May 31st 1996, the deadline fixed by the President.

The B.J.P. Govt. says that it is confident of proving its majority in the crucial trial of strength in the House. The Third Front and the Congress too are asserting that they will bring down the Vajpayee Govt. by voting against its motion seeking the Confidence of the House.

If the numerical strengths of the parties are any indication, there seems to be no doubt about the imminent fall of the BJP Govt. But, having got its long cherished opportunity to form the Govt. at the Centre, the BJP is leaving no stone unturned for ensuring the continuance of its Govt. beyond May 31st, 1996.

As a first step, Vajpayee has stated that the issue of Ram Mandir at Ayodhya is not on the priority list of his Govt. He has also told that the policies of the previous Government would not be changed.

Vajpayee's popular image of being accommodative on sensitive issues like the special status of Jammu & Kashmir, and uniform civil code and his rapport with the opposition leaders like P.V. Narasimha Rao and Biju Patnaik are the factors which could influence a few of the MP's outside the B.J.P. and its allies to give a chance to the Govt. to survive. Incidentally, it would be in their own interest also, as it would ensure their own continuance as members of the Lok Sabha.

But, it is interesting to speculate as to what might happen in the event of the fall of the B.J.P. Govt. Despite the assurance of the Congress to support the Third Front, the President may extend his invitation to P.V. Narasimha Rao, the leader of the second largest party in the Lok Sabha to form the Govt. In that case, it is quite possible that the Congress may agree to form the Govt. hoping to be supported by the Third Front. The B.J.P. might not be too eager to bring down the Congresss Ministry for strategic reasons. For between the Congress and the Third Front, the B.J.P. considers the former as the lesser evil. Moreover, the popularity of the Congress Govt. having diminished in the recent past, it will be to the B.J.P's advantage to allow that party to become more unpopular by being in power for a few more months. Alternatively, the Congress may decline the invitation and renew its pledge to support the Third Front paving the way for the President to invite H.D. Deve Gowda to form the Govt.

The chances of a reasonably long survival of the Govt. in either case seem to be very remote. The reasons for this prediction are not far to seek. The first is the difficulty in keeping together the Third Front which is a conglomerate of too many parties with the Janta Dal at its head. The second is the bitter opposition of the CPI(M) and a few leaders of the J.D. to have anything to do with the Congress and particularly with P.V. Narasimha Rao. The third is that the Congress could withdraw its support anytime on any issue as it has done earlier to the Charan Singh Govt. and the Chandra Shekhar Government.

In fact, a coalition Govt. formed by the Third Front and the Congress would have a better chance of surviving for some reasonable time of two to three years. If they are keen on keeping the B.J.P. out of power, the parties concerned should first tone down their criticism of each other and agree upon a minimum common programme, deleting therefrom all controversial points.

If the parties maintain their irreconcilable stands, a midterm election for the Lok Sabha within this year or early next year would become inevitable. Following the precedants set by N. Sanjeeva Reddy and R. Venkataraman by dissolving the Lok Sabha on the advice of the then Prime Ministers, Charan Singh and Chandra Shekhar although they were in a woeful minority, Dr. Shankar Dayal Sharma too may dissolve the Lok Sabha if the head of a minority Govt. advises him to do so either after the fall of the Govt. or before the imminent fall of the Govt.

Another point to be noted is that there is no guarantee that even in the next General Election, any party would get an absolute majority in the House. Therefore, the parties should sit together and work out a solution for such an eventuality even before the elections are held.

The claims and counter-claims of the parties, particularly, the B.J.P. and the Third Front about the people's mandate being in their favour are meaningless in view of the following facts. On an average, 50% to 55% of the voters only have exercised their franchise. Several hundreds of thousands of voters including this writer could not vote as their names were not found on the Voters' lists for some reason or the other.

The glaring anamolies mentioned below also are worth noting. The B.J.P. secured 160 seats by polling less than 25% of the votes cast. Moreover its performance in the states like Kerala, Andhra Pradesh and West Bengal was extremely poor. The Congress got only 136 seats although it has polled more than 30% of the votes cast. The N.F.- L.F. combine's tally of 111 includes those of several parties like the J.D., S.P., C.P.I.(M) and C.P.I. which, strangely enough, found themselves ranged against one another while extending their support to some parties in a few States. While the C.P.I. supported the DMK, the CPI(M) and J.D. supported the M.D.M.K. in Tamil Nadu. Similarly, in Andhra Pradesh, the CPI and CPI(M) threw their lot with the TDP (Naidu) whereas the JD supported the NTRTDP (Lakshmi Parvathi).

Turning to the voting pattern, it is difficult to say whether a party has won on a positive vote or a negative vote. For instance, in Tamil Nadu it is widely believed that the voters gave a thumping victory to the D.M.K.-led electoral alliance because of their anger against the Jayalalitha Govt.'s attitude and performance over the past five years. In the same way, if the Lok Sabha election results could be interpreted as a disapproval of the Congress policy, how could it be called a positive mandate for the B.J.P.? Moreover, how could the Congress have emerged as the second largest party with 136 seats giving a particularly good account of itself in Andhra Pradesh, Orissa and Himachal Pradesh? Obviously this proves that the local issues and the relative strengths of the various parties in the states have inluenced the voters in the pattern of their voting.

In Madhya Pradesh, the relatively poor performance of the Congress could be attributed to the formation of Madhya Pradesh Vikas Party by Madhav Rao Scindia and the Indira Congress (T) by Arjun Singh. They might not have gained much as M.P. Vikas Party could get only 3 seats and Arjun Singh was even defeated in the Satna Lok Sabha Constituency. But they have succeeded in depleting the strength of the Congress substantially.

As for the commitment to policies of secularism and social justice" on the basis of which the Third Front is attacking the B.J.P. and to a lesser extent, the Congress, one should note as to how George Fernandes, once considered as a firebrand socialist finds himself in alliance with the B.J.P. now. Many erstwhile J.D. members like Charanjit Yadav, and Bidhuri are in the Congress right now. People will not be surprised if many more would follow their example if it serves their own interests.

Maybe, the efforts of the B.J.P. in wooing the regional parties and a few members of the Congress would succeed and the Govt. would survive the trial of strength by "manipulation" instead of "horse-trading" although neither of them can be called as `honest means'. Even if the crisis blows over now a similar crisis could occur in the future also. Therefore, the parties should strive to incorporate a clause in the Constitution making it obligatory on the part of the parties to allow the single largest party, or a coalition of parties (if it is formed beofre the elections) to run the Govt. for a minimum period of 2 to 3 years without toppling it. This will ensure reasonable stability to the Government and avoidance of holding mid term elections too frequently.

11

Congress Fiasco in Chindwara

People were not surprised by the defeat of the Congress party in the Pubjab Assembly elections. For, it was being widely predicted for quite some time. However, the margin by which the party was defeated has surprised many.

The dissidents in the Party are blaming Sitaram Kesri's policies for the party's poor showing. The replacement of Harcharan Singh Brar with Rajinder Kaur Bhattal as the Chief Minister just before the Assembly elections and the fielding of the so-called hawala-tainted leaders, Kamal Nath and Buta Singh as the party's candidates in the Chindwara and Ropar byelections to the Lok Sabha are being cited by them as the main reasons wihch have alienated many traditional supporters of the Party.

As for the byelections to the State Assemblies, the Congress should feel happy with its tally of three out of the 14 seats. This is no mean achievement, considering the strength of the parties like the D.M.K., T.D.P., B.J.P. and S.P. which were pitted against it. Moreover, no other party has won more than two seats. But, the Congress must have been greatly worried about its defeat in the byelections to the Lok Sabha, particularly when it is said to be toying with the idea of forming its own Government at the Centre.

The reasons for the rejection of the party by the electorate in these elections are not so simple as it is made out to be. The election of Madhavrao Scindia and Kalp Nath Rai to the Lok Sabha in the 1996 General election disproves the assertion of some that all leaders, hawala-tainted or facing criminal charges, would be rejected by the electorate.

The general feeling in Punjab is that the Congress Government had let loose a regime of police atrocities in its zeal to eliminate terrorism from the State. While the Congress party tried to bank upon the restoration of normalcy in the State, the Shiromani Akali Dal (Badal), B.J.P. combine has effectively countered it by labelling the Government as corrupt and by reminding the people of the sufferings some of them had to undergo at the hands of the police.

The results of the Punjab Assembly elections bear a close comparison to the results of the post-Emergency elections to the Lok Sabha in 1977 when the Congress party was routed particularly in the Northern States, although many people acknowledged privately that the Emergency had brought about a strict discipline which was never heard of earlier or since then in our country. What was disliked by the people in both these cases was the sense of fear coupled with a feeling of a loss of freedom experienced by them during those periods.

The cases of harassment and persecution of the people need not be too many. Even, only a few could also rouse the feelings of the people against the Government, if they are well publicised. In the two elections cited above, the people appeared to have taken the earliest opportunity to vote out the ruling party, in spite of its achievements in certain administrative and development areas.

This mood of the people of Punjab must have been the main reason for the ignominious defeat of Buta Singh by such a wide margin of more than one lakh votes. Of course, there are other reasons too like the in-fighting of the leaders of the party, the poll pact of the SAD(B) and BJP and the failure of the Congress to forge an alliance with parties like CPM and the BSP.

In Nagaur Lok Sabha constituency, Ram Niwas Mirdha of the Congress party had lost to Bhanu Prakash Mirdha of the BJP by a very slender margin of about 1,000 votes. It is reported that Bhanu Prakash Mirdha had fought the election on the BJP ticket after having been denied the ticket from the Congress.

In this case, it would have been very difficult for anyone to have predicted as to which of them had a better chance to win. Maybe, the Congress party's attempts to dislodge the BJP Government in Rajasthan by encouraging the dissidents of that party have weaned away some of its supporters to the other side.

The byelelction in Baghpat Lok Sabha constituency was caused by the resignation of Ajit Singh after having been elected on the Congress ticket in May last. He has now contested as the candidate of Bharatiya Kisan Kamgar Party and won the election by a large margin. He was left with no other course to enter the Lok Sabha, as he would have anyway forfeited his Lok Sabha seat as per the rules of the anti-defection act, after having left the Congress party on the eve of the Assembly elections in U.P.

The Congress had met with its worst fate in the Lok Sabha by-election in Chindwara constituency. In fact, this seat was won by Alka Nath, the wife of Kamal Nath on the Congress ticket in May 1996 general election. But she resigned her seat unnecessarily. The only reason that one could surmise in forcing this byelection is that Kamal Nath wanted to prove his popularity and clout in this Constituency, once again. Having represented the people of that constituency for 16 long years since 1980, he must have thought that he could win an election in that constituency hands down, at any time.

In the last general election he was denied the Congress ticket in the wake of the hawala scam in which he was alleged to be involved along with some others. However, in view of his popularity in the constituency, the ticket was given to his wife. At that time, he claimed that he could ensure the victory of his wife without any help from the other leaders of the Congress. Indeed, he had proved his popularity by getting her elected, although with a small majority.

May be, he has tried to test his popularity once too often by contesting in this by-election now. Indeed, the defeat of Kamal Nath in this election should teach a lesson to all the politicians so that they should never take their electorate for granted.

No doubt, a section of the electorate in Chindwara would not have liked a by-election being forced to take place without any valid reason apparantly other than to satisfy the vanity of a political leader. Perhaps some of them have switched over their preference to his opponent. Moreover, he had to face this time a top leader of the BJP in Madhya Pradesh, Sundarlal Patwa who had proved to be a hard nut to crack.

However much one may think that he has served his constituency he/she should not feel that his/her victory is always assured in that constituency. For, many other factors like the changing political climate, the strength of the opposition parties, the percentage of voter turn out, the weather conditions etc. could also very well influence the result of an election.

When K. Kamaraj, the then President of the Congress party was injured in a car accident during the 1967 general election, he was reported to have said that he would win the election to the Tamil Nadu Assembly from his home constituency, Virudhunagar, even lying down on his bed. But, he was defeated by a virtual new entrant to politics, P. Srinivasan as the D.M.K. candidate.

Similarly, the defeat of Indira Gandhi in the Rai-Bareilly Lok Sabha constituency in 1977 and that of Jayalalitha in the Tamil Nadu Assembly elections in May 96 should act as eye openers to those who feel over-confident about their victory in an election.

The Congress should have remembered the proverb, "A bird in hand is worth two in the bush" and dissuaded Alka Nath from resigning her seat in the Lok Sabha. Thereby, it would have avoided its loss of one Lok Sabha seat as well as a loss of face besides the needless expenditure from the Govt. exchequer on the by-election. Incidentally, while there is a clamour for increasing the representation of women in the Legislatures, the resignation of Alka Nath has resulted in the reduction of the strength of the woman members in the Lok Sabha.

12

Explore Permanent Solution for Political Crises

Although the Deve Gowda Government was voted out in the Lok Sabha, Sitaram Kesri's objectives still remain unfulfilled. For, neither the Congress is in a position to form a Government nor the United Front has disintegrated.

It is no wonder, therefore, that many of the Congress MPs are very unhappy with their party President for having precipitated the crisis and exposed the party to a scathing criticism from several sides.

The President handled the crisis in an appropriate manner by asking Deve Gowda to seek a vote of confidence in the Lok Sabha instead of asking him to resign as soon as the Congress Party withdrew its support to his Government. If the latter course was followed, the problem would have been further complicated.

The hopes of the B.J.P. to form the Government by mustering the support of some of the parties of the U.F. are also belied. If, indeed, those parties had offered their support to the BJP, their credentials as secular parties would have been shattered.

Undoubtedly, there is a point in the argument of the Congress Party that if a party with 45 members in the Lok Sabha could lead the coalition Government, why should not the Congress Party having about 140 seats in the Lok Sabha try to do the same. But, the Congress party should have staked its claim soon after the elections in May last year and before the formation of the U.F. Government.

At that time, the party had meekly accepted the interpretation of the electoral results as a rejection of the party by the people. Moreover, even if it wanted to form the Government, it is doubtful whether its efforts would have succeeded in view of the antipathy of the C.P.I., C.P.I. (M) and J.D. for the Congress. Even the T.M.C., T.D.P. and D.M.K. were quite bitter with the Congress soon after the Lok Sabha elections.

Therefore, many people felt that the unconditional support extended by the Congress for the formation of the U.F. Government was the best option available to it for upholding its avowed policy of secularism by keeping the B.J.P. out of power. If the party was shrewd, it could have joined the Government. It could also have asked for its representation on the U.F. Steering Committee to deliberate on the policy matters. But it has failed to do so.

May be, it was hoping that the U.F. would split and thereby give it an opportunity to form its own Government with the support of some of the constituents of the U.F. When such a split has not taken place even after ten months, it appears that the Congress President and a section of the party became quite impatient.

The unsavoury remarks of Sitaram Kesri about Deve Gowda are not in good taste. Incidentally, stung by those remarks perhaps, Deve Gowda appropriately gave it back to Kesri, while replying to the debate on his motion of confidence in the Lok Sabha. His supporters as well as his critics were surprised alike as few people have credited him with such devastating debating skills.

No doubt, the U.F. is justified in saying that the demand of the Congress to change its leader is unfair..But, unfortunately, some of the Opposition Parties (which form part of the U.F. now) are also guilty of making such demands when they stated that they would support the Government of the Congress if the party removed its leaders, Rajiv Gandhi and P.V. Narasimha Rao when they were leading their respective Governments.

The Congress should remember that after the split in the party in 1969, Indira Gandhi headed a minority Government supported by the C.P.I. and the D.M.K. for nearly two years. But the Congress Party has not reciprocated to the other parties with its unstinted support. In fact, it has acquired a bad reputation for being unrealiable as a supporting party after having brought down the Governments of Charan Singh, Chandra Shekhar and Deve Gowda.

Though it is not well publicised, the B.J.P. is also not far behind in this respect as it has toppled the Government of V.P. Singh at the Centre and that of Mayawati during her earlier stint in Uttar Pradesh by withdrawing its support.

In the light of this background, even if the Congress Party or the B.J.P. succeeds in forming a Government with the help of some of the constituents of the U.F., how could it hope to ensure that those parties would not pay it back in the same coin and ditch its Government after some time? It is also doubtful whether the Congress could be trusted to give its support to another U.F. Government, headed by a new leader for a reasonably long time. Unless a coalition is formed before an election, it will be viewed by the public as opportunistic. Moreover, it cannot be deemed to have the sanction or approval of the electorate.

If the present stalemate continues, a mid-term poll will become inevitable. Not only such an exercise would cost a lot of money but also there is no guarantee that a hung Lok Sabha would not come into being once again.

Although some people keep on saying that the era of single party governments is over and the age of coalition governments has arrived, our experience with coalition governments is not quite encouraging, if the sordid political dramas played in U.P. and elsewhere provide any indication.

In the year 1993, in U.P. the S.P.-B.S.P. alliance emerged as the single largest group in the Assembly by winning a few more seats than the B.J.P. But none of the parties secured an absolute majority. The S.P.-B.S.P. alliance formed a coalition Government with Mulayam Singh Yadav as the Chief Minister with the support of the Congress and J.D. But due to internal differences, the B.S.P. withdrew from the coalition and brought down the Government. Soon after, with the support of the B.J.P., the B.S.P. formed a Government with Mayawati as the Chief Minister. Even that Government did not last long as the BJP withdrew its support to the BSP Government within four and a half months of its formation.

When the Assembly elections were held in October, last, after a long spell of President's rule, a hung Assembly came into being once again in spite of some changes in the electoral alliances of the parties. The stalemate continued for nearly six months more with no party or a group of parties being able to form a stable Government.

Although the B.S.P.-Congress alliance had emerged as the third largest group with only about 100 seats in a House of 425 seats, the BSP was adament that Mayawati should be made the Chief Minister. The Congress Party's appeal to the U.F. to support the B.S.P. in forming a Government proved futile because of the hostility between the S.P. and the B.S.P. The BJP's efforts to gain the support of the other parties for securing a majority too failed miserably.

Finally, in March this year (1997), the BSP and the BJP have arrived at an understanding to form the Government with Mayawati as the Chief Minister for the first six months. Later, the leader of the BJP legislature party, Kalyan Singh would take over as the Chief Minister for the next six months. The ministry will have equal representation from the two parties although BJP's strength in the Assembly is nearly three times that of the BSP. The situation will be reviewed at the end of one year.

The people fail to understand how the erstwhile opponents have come together to form a Government now. Is it not an opportunistic alliance? Are the plitical parties justified in coming to power by any means for sharing the spoils of the office? Moreover, is there a guarantee that this experiment would succeed now particularly in view of their alliance having failed to click not very long ago?

The experience at the Centre too is not different with regard to the coalition Governments of Morarji Desai and V.P. Singh.

Therefore, to suit the conditions in our country, the Constitution should be amended suitably to ensure the formation of a Government by a single party or a coalition of parties (formed before the elections) even with a hung Assembly or hung Lok Sabha coming into being and its stability for a reasonable period.

This can perhaps be done by stipulating that a Government formed by a party by virtue of being the single largest party shall be allowed to function for a minimum period of three years.

13

Desecration of B. R. Ambedkar's Statue

Any right thinking person would not hesitate to condemn the reported act of desecration of the statue of Babasaheb Ambedkar at the Ramabai Ambedkar Nagar in north-east Mumbai. The Government of Maharashtra should spare no effort in tracing and bringing to book the person/persons responsible for that wretched and shameful act. If the aim of the culprits was to express their opposition to what Ambedkar had professed or stood for, they followed a most cowardly and detestable way to do so.

It is unfortunate that 10 people were killed and 29 injured (as per newspaper reports) in the police firing on the people while they were demonstrating angrily on the roads by pelting stones at the passing vehicles to protest against the desecration of the statue on the 11th of July 1997. The very next day, a bandh was called by some political parties as a protest against the police firing. Again violence erupted in parts of the city and the police resorted to firing in which two more persons were killed and several others injured.

It is a pity that the political leaders, instead of trying to defuse the tension are trying to make political capital out of such unfortunate happenings. For fear of losing their votes, they are not saying even one word against the unseemly and disproportionate reaction of the people to the desecration of the statue.

It is a known fact that the police are, by and large, high handed, hasty and indiscriminate. The recent incidents of the beating up of Massey Martin and the killing of two business men in Connaught Place in Delhi are perhaps only two of the many such dastardly acts being committed by the police day-in and day-out in the name of maintaining law and order in all parts of the country.

Whether there was justification for the police firing or not will be known only after the judicial probe ordered into the incident is completed. But generally, by the time a judicial probe is completed, the incident will be forgotten by many people.

As usual, during the strike, several ugly incidents took place. It was reported that the houses of Chhagan Bhujbal and Madhukar Rao Pichhad, leaders of the Congress Party in the Legislative Council and Assembly respectively were attacked and Ramdas Athavale, a RPI Leader physically assaulted by some miscreants. The Congress leaders accused the Shiv Sena for the attacks. They stated that the Government did not like their criticism of the police firing.

It is a wonder why the political leaders indulge in accusing one another whenever any unfortunate incident occurs instead of trying to analyse the matter impassionately and trying to defuse the tension. If they are responsible leaders, they should sit together to consider what steps should be taken to prevent recurrence of such incidents.

No doubt, the desecration of the statue was reprehensible. But was the reaction of the people of the colony right and reasonable? For instance, can anybody justify violence or arson by a person and his friends in retaliation of some senseless fellows' abusive words aimed at them? After all, the reaction or retaliation must be reasonable. Otherwise, the person/

persons cannot be sympathised with or their actions condoned. From this point of view, the remarks of Mayawati justifying the behaviour of the mob would not serve the cause of fostering good-will between the people of the different castes.

If this trend is encouraged, any miscreant would be able to create a caste war at any time by resorting to some mischief to hurt the feelings of the people of one caste or the other and the consequences thereof could be quite dangerous to the nation.

It is unfortunate that Dadasaheb Ambedkar is being projected as a leader of Dalits only by some people. It appears that in the last few years, the Dalits were made to think that it falls to their lot to preserve the image and importance of that leader.

But the real fact is that Ambedkar has already secured an important place in our country's history as the Architect of our Constitution. He had also served as a Cabinet Minister in the Nehru Government for some time. It is to be noted that his statue is the most prominent one among those of the other leaders in the premises of the Parliament House. In all the Doordarshan telecasts of the Parliament news, the statue of Ambedkar is quite rightly shown to the viewers. This was being done even much before the people of a few castes have taken upon themselves as their duty to glorify him in the recent past.

Many statues of Ambedkar were already installed in prominent places in several cities like Hyderabad and some other towns. Quite fittingly for the role played by him, many colonies, stadiums, colleges etc. have been named after him. In fact, he is and should be looked upon as a national leader and not as a leader of the people of a few castes only.

Therefore, the leaders should advise the people not to get excited and provoked by the acts of miscreants and trouble mongers. They should be advised not to give vent to their anger on such matters. They should be made to realise how much they are suffering in such cases. In the case of the unfortunate incident of the desecration of the statue, the people of the colony could have reported to the nearby police station or to the collector or to the Minister. They could also have brought it to the attention of the newspaper Journalists and T.V. reporters. If such an action was taken, the unfortunate loss of life could have been avoided.

It is regrettable that some people seem to take a pleasure in denigrating the leaders of the past. Even Gandhi is not spared by them. The best way to tackle such critics is perhaps to ignore them or when it is really felt necessary, the concerned people could give a rejoinder to such criticism.

Also a concerted effort should be made to discourage the installation of statues of the leaders in public places. For, in most cases the statues are not taken proper care of. Often, crows and other birds are found to perch on such statues. Some statues do not even bear a resembalance to the persons whose replicas they are supposed to be. They could also become targets of the fury of the mobs during mass agitations. Miscreants could desecrate them to create trouble in Society.

If at all statues are to be installed, they should be located in guarded premises only. As far as possible, people should try to perpetuate the memory of their leaders by constructing a school or a library or a hospital or any such thing useful to the people in their daily lives rather than by installing their statues.

The recent controversy about the installation of a statue of a caste leader in Tamil Nadu and the violence that it had resulted in should serve as an eye opener to all the people in this respect. The people should also take note of how the statues of Lenin, hailed as one of the greatest leaders till a few years ago, were removed in several countries of the world in the wake of the break-up of the Soviet Union and the fall of the Communist Government there.

14

Governments and Criticism

Criticism can be classified as constructive or negative. The former is always welcome as it produces a healthy impact and leaves not trace of bitterness. On the other hand, negative criticism often tends to be acrimonious and serves no purpose but to generate an ill-feeling.

In India, people enjoy a very high degree of freedom of expression and freedom of press. Some criticisms we read in papers and hear in speeches make us wonder whether these precious privileges and rights are being used in a responsible and useful manner.

If the Government has a huge majority in the State Assembly or Parliament, the critics would say that the Government is functioning with its "Steam roller" majority. They even go to the extent of suggesting that such a huge majority for a single party is not conducive to democracy. On the other hand, if the Government has got a narrow majority or has to depend on one or more parties for its continuance in Office, these critics jump to their feet and shout from the house tops that the Government has no moral right to continue in power and demand the immediate resignation of the Government.

If the Government hesitates to recommend the dissolution

of an Assembly or the Lok Sabha, the critics point an accusing finger attributing this hesitation to a desire to cling to power at any cost. But if such a dissolution is ordered and a fresh election called for, they will again condemn the Government in the strongest words for "arbitrarily" taking recourse to such an action. Some, even make no bones about passing pungent and unsavoury remarks about the attitutde of the Governor or President for accepting the advice of a Chief Minister or a Prime Minister.

Before the elections, these cressendras predict the doom of the Government and when the ruling party is returned to power, they invent all stories of malpractices and irregularities as a scape-goat for their predictions to have gone wrong. For example, to suggest that in any constituency some thousands of names of voters who according to them, would have voted agianst a candidate have been deleted from the voters' lists and several thousands of names of other people supporting the candidate have been included in the voters' list is nothing short of a wild and fantastic imagination. Can any one suggest the names of some thousands of common people who would certainly vote for him or her? And if so, how could those names be included in the lists?

They raise the bogey of chemicals used on the ballot papers or misleading religious symbols used by the parties. They say that the people being innocent and illiterate, are misled easily by vain and false promises. Perhaps, with such presumptions about the people, they hope to raise doubts in the minds of the people by making such preposterous and absurd allegations.

If one Officer is promoted ignoring the seniority of another on the basis of merit or other administrative considerations, these critics would immediately invent a political motive for that. If the seniority is strictly observed, the Government will be accused of lacking in boldness and being too much status - quo minded. If any discordant note comes to the surface in the working of a cabinet, however trivial it might be, the critics paint a grim picture showing the Government work as having come to a standstill.

If an anticipated Cabinet reshuffle does not materialise, they charge the Prime Minister or Chief Minister with weakness. When such a reshuffle takes place, they again accuse the Prime Minister or Chief Minister of having reduced somebody's importance or cutting some other to size or strengthening his or her own position.

If a Governor refuses to oblige a doubtful aspirant with an invitation to form the Government, these critics would immediately try to locate the invisible strings through which the Central Government is manipulating the Governor. In their view, the Governors, at any rate most of them, are just puppets lacking in grit, stamina and self assertiveness. They forget that a Governor is in most cases a person of great prestige, talent, ability and an indpendant mind and aspires for little at the cost of self respect. Any Governor worth his salt would refuse to dance to the tunes of the Central Government if its instructions clearly violate his constitutional responsibilities.

If a court gives a judgement which goes counter to the Government, they praise the judiciary as the only hope left for the democracy to be saved. But if such a judgement goes in favour of the Government much to the chagrin of these critics and self styled protectors of democracy, they immediately brand the judiciary as being subservient to the Government.

These critics presume to have a ready made solution for even the most complex and intricate problem of a State, be it political, economic, social, scientific or religious. They always condemn the Government with bell, book and candle for everything they do or don't do. They would like the people to believe that they could correctly suggest what should be done in the case of "Rabat episode" or "Kashmir problem", "Bangla Desh", "Communal flare-up", "Agriculturists' agitation"

"Government employees' or students' strike" or any other problem. If the Government takes a soft line and tries for a peaceful and amicable settlement, these critics charge the Government with pusillanimity and ambivalance. On the other hand, if sterner measures are employed for bringing the situation under control, the Government will be branded as repressive, inhuman and authoritarian.

To charge the Government with incompetence, inefficency corruption, vacillation, red tapism, nepotism etc. has become the fashion of the day. Some cynics and prophets of doom suggest that only a military take-over may put an end to many of the present day ills besetting the country. The happenings in Pakistan since the Coup de'etat staged by General Ayub Khan in 1958 and particularly those of the past few months in Gen. Yahya Khan's regime should act as an eye-opener to them. It will be like a miracle if any country could return to civilian rule after once the Military takes over the Administration. It is only to be hoped that these critics would have drawn their lessons and shed their illusions about the virtues of Military rule.

These critics pretend to be the only right thinking people wishing the good of the country. But by exhibiting such a frivolous attitude in critisizing the Governments always, the critics are setting at naught the very values they are ostensibly trying to preserve. They will do well to pause and think before offering voceferous criticism in strong words, at times reaching the stage of being vulgar and vituperative.

It is not intended to defend here all that the Governments are doing. There may be some omissions and commissions creeping into their work now and then. At times, even big blunders might be committed and malpractices resorted to. Such issues must be picked up specifically and commented upon in a constructive way suggesting ways for remedying the same. Criticism should be proportional to the magnitude of the points at issue and should be tempered with sobreity and reasonableness. If in every case the critics condemn the Government in the same words, people will get disgusted with such criticism and in course of time, they will tend to ignore even justified criticism as being motivated and scornful.

Governments also should take careful note of all such constructive criticism from whichever quarter it might be offered and should not hesitate to set a thing right if anything has gone wrong without considering that it would be "infra dig" or a loss of face for them to do so. Governments having been returned to power with people's mandate have great responsibilities to discharge. Their performance will be ultimately judged by how much they have improved the people's condition rather than their statistics of the number of constitution amendments, abrortive measures for radical reforms or high sounding but futile speeches.

(This article was written in around 1972)

15

Suggestions for Speedy Dispensation of Justice

There is a general feeling that in the present judicial system, the dispensation of Justice involves a long process. Some of the reasons for this are as follows:

(1) There are too many cases to be dealt with due to a phenomenal increase in the litigation. (2) The number of Judges, Magistrates, Munsiffs and other Judicial officers are too few to deal with so many cases. (3) Quite a few lawyers take up too many cases at a time to be able to study and prepare for the hearings on the stipulated dates. Therefore, they seek adjournment of their cases on one pretext or the other. (4) The party deriving advantage by prolonging a case manouvers through its lawyer for getting the case adjourned as often as possible.

There are many instances of cases prolonging for decades. At times by the time, a case is disposed of, the original litigants might not be existing and their successors would have continued the litigation.

Another thing causing a lot of concern to the public in general and the litigants in particular is the ever mounting cost of legal proceedings. The fee charged by the lawyers is generally too high. They have to be paid for filing the case and later for every hearing whether they argue the case or merely ask for an adjournment. Depending on their own demand and the litigants' urgency, the lawyers fix their own fees, sometimes running into astronomical figures. If it is justified by saying, that the lawyers charging higher fee can expound the case better and the chances of their clients winning the case are better, does it not amount to admitting that the richer litigant has a better chance of winning his case? It is no exaggeration to say that the courts, at any rate, higher judicial courts are almost out of reach of the common man, what-with the exorbitant cost involved in going there for justice.

In many cases, it may be quite obvious that one party is the aggrieved and the other the aggressor. Or, let us say that one party is innocent and the other guilty. Even in such cases, lawyers are prepared to represent either side, if the concerned party is willing to pay their fee. Here, some interesting questions such as the following arise in the minds of the thinking public.

Are the lawyers meant to interprete the law before the Judge/Judicial Officer or twist the facts and otherwise juggle the law points with the sole intention of winning the cases for their clients, whether they are convinced about their clients' being right or wrong? If the lawyers indulge in such unhealthy practices, what are the remedies available to set them right? Is it necessary for a Judge/Judicial Officer to follow a precedent quoted by a lawyer, whether the Judge/Judicial Officer agrees with that precedent in the circumstances of the present case or not? Are Lawyers always necessary to interprete and argue a case? Can't the Judge/Judicial Officer decide a case on the basis of the presentation of a case by a litigant in his own words in writing or orally?

In order to relieve the poorer section of the litigants of their financial burden in pursuing their cases, some people have been advocating that free legal advice should be made available to them. But it is not known how it can be implemented. Where from the funds would be provided to pay the lawyers giving free legal service to the poor? How could one establish whether someone is really poor to be eligible to get such free legal advice? What will be the calibre of the lawyers who would opt for giving legal advice to the poor, getting a fixed remuneration instead of setting up their own private practices? What interest would they take in the cases of such clients, without a stake in winning or losing the case?

Another suggestion that has been made was that a lawyer should charge a certain percentage of the money got by his client by way of a court award. The lawyer should not charge any fee if his client loses the case. The flaws in this suggestion are too obvious. Some of them are mentioned below:

(1) All the cases do not involve an award of money to the winning party. (2) Even if an award is given to a party in a case, the opposite party may appeal to a higher court and as such the money might not be paid to the party. (3) In cases involving landed property etc, the determination of the actual benefit derived by the winning party may become problematical. (4) The lawyers will become too choosy in taking up cases. In some cases, they may sincerely believe that their cases are good but may end up losing them. If this happens, the Lawyers stand to lose considerably due to waste of their time and not being compensated for their efforts.

We have adopted the present Judicial system on the model of the British Judicial system. Perhaps, the Judicial system is quite similar in many other countries. But, in view of the above points, the existing system needs a thorough review. It should also be changed to suit the requirements of the general public. The following suggestions may be considered to achieve the above objective.

(1) Let a qualified lawyer be posted in every village or a group of 2 to 3 villages as a local law officer. He should be empowered to deal with the cases within those villages and give his verdict.

(2) In the towns and cities, there should be one or two such law officers for every Municipal/Corporation ward.

(3) A senior Judicial officer should be appointed to cover

the jurisdication of six to ten local law officers with his Headquarters located within the area of his jurisdiction.

(4) At each district Head Quarters or town or city, a District Court should be located with powers to deal with appeals over the judgements of the lower court.

(5) In state capitals, there should be High Courts with the requisite number of Judges depending on the work load, to deal with cases involving State Government Legislation and a few categorised cases as appeals against the Judgement of the District Courts in which the value of property involved is more than Rs. 10 crores or the sentence in criminal cases exceeding 10 years imprisonment.

The Supreme Court in the Capital city of our country should have special benches at least in four more cities so that no one has to travel more than, say, 500 km to seek a judicial remedy in the Supreme Court. This Court should deal with cases between two State Governments and the cases between State Governments and Central Government, and institutions and individuals involved in litigation with the Central Government only. For interpretation of constitutional matters, a special bench of five Judges can be constituted. These Judges may be appointed from a panel of names of retired Chief Justices and renowned scholars in law and permanant Judges of the Supreme Court. This bench should be reconstituted once in five years. During this term, if a vacancy arises temporarily or permanently the same should be filled up immediately from the panel of names submitted by the Chief Justice of the Supreme Court.

The salary structure, promotion and transfers of these Judges and the staff to assist them etc can be codified suitably. The litigants should be required to pay only a nominal Court fee. Justice should be rendered almost free of charge. The salaries of the Judges and staff should be borne by the Government as in the case of certain other service departments.

Of course, certain defects could be shown in this system also. But such defects are existing in the existing system also, perhaps to a greater degree.

16

Arbitration to Resolve Disputes

On the 11th & 12th of November 1994, a seminar was organised in New Delhi by the Indian Society of arbitration for "an exchange of new ideas on International Arbitration". From the 6th to 10th of March 1995, an International conference on construction Management was held in New Delhi by the Central Board of Irrigation and Power. In both of the seminars, several papers were presented on procedures of arbitration, hurdles faced and methods to get over them. This shows the increasing recognition of arbitration as a means of resolving disputes between business and commercial organisations, in the recent times. Therefore, it may be appropriate to share some ideas with the readers on this subject, limiting its scope to disputes to be resolved between parties within our country.

The arbitration act 1940 was enacted with the object of getting the disputes between parties resolved expeditiously. Incidentally this procedure was also expected to reduce the number of cases going before the various courts, to a large extent. But in actual practice, what is generally happening with regard to the arbitration process is perhaps best described by Justice D.A. Desai in the following words.

"Interminable, time consuming complex and expensive procedures impelled Jurists to search for an alternative forum, less formal, more effective and speedy for solution of disputes avoiding procedural claptrap and this led them to arbitration

Act, 1940. However, the way in which the proceedings under the Act are conducted and without an exception challenged in courts, has made lawyers laugh and legal philosophers weep. Experience shows and law reports bear ample testimony that the proceedings under the Act have become highly technical accompanied by unending prolixity, at every stage providing a legal trap to the unwary. Informal forum chosen by the parties for expeditious disposal of their disputes has by the decisions of the courts been clothed with 'legalise' of unforeseeable complexity. (AIR 1981 PAGE 2076 S.C.).

For the arbitration procedure to become effective, certain concrete measures have to be taken. First of all, the legal personnel - be it retired Judges or practising lawyers - should be excluded or at least discouraged from taking part in the arbitration proceedings. For, they tend to make them look like the court proceedings. Often, legal intricacies are given more importance than the real issues at stake. There by, a lot of time is consumed and also confusion created.

Generally, their fees are also very high. The lawyers being busy with their normal work in the courts would not give due attention to the matters pending before the arbitrators. Because of lack of preparation and also their limitations of understanding certain issues of specialised fields, they would keep on seeking adjournments on one pretext or the other, thereby letting the arbitration proceedings prolong for many years, at times. The law of arbitration has fixed the tenure of an arbitrator as four months only with a view to expediting the disposal of a case in the shortest possible time. The provision for the extension of the tenure by a period of another four months was perhaps made to take care of the exigencies due to unforeseen reasons like the arbitrator or the key personnel of the parties falling sick or for collection of certain relevant data etc. But, now-a-days this provision is being made use of as a matter of routine for extending the tenure of the arbitrators each time by four months, repeatedly any number of times.

Another important point is that in certain matters of

technical nature, the retired judges and lawyers are often finding it difficult to properly understand the issues in dispute, in spite of the best efforts of the parties to brief them thoroughly.

Therefore it is suggested that the arbitrators should be retired persons from the profession connected with the subject matter of the disputes. For instance, it is reasonable to expect that a dispute arising out of a building construction project can be understood better by a person with experience and knowledge in building construction. Many times, the lawyers and retired judges are not able to understand such technical words as 'deflection', 'uniformly distributed load', 'point loads', 'trusses', 'prestressed concrete', 'design', etc. Similarly, for resolving a dispute with regard to the accounts in a Company, a reputed Chartered Accountant could be a better choice for appointment as an arbitrator than a person from any other profession. The parties should also employ professionals in the concerned field to present their respective cases before the arbitrators, if they would not like to do it themselves. The duration of the proceedings should not last more than four months. In rare cases, the extension of the term may be permitted by another four months. If the proceedings need more time for completion because of extra ordinary conditions, the term may be further extended by another four months. The proceedings should not be allowed to continue for more than one year in any case referred for arbitration.

For the arbitraton proceedings to be expedited within the time frame suggested above and to make them less expensive a few norms suggested below may be considered for adoption.

The arbitrators should be selected from a place which is quite near to the places of the litigant parties. For instance, if the parties are at Delhi, the arbitrators should be selected from Delhi itself. This will facilitate the avoidance of large expense on travel and reduction in journey time. The fees of the arbitrators should have an upper limit of, say, Rs. 2,000/- per each hearing of one day or part thereof. In addition, the arbitrators should be reimbursed with the actual charges incurred by them for travel to the venue of arbitration, typing etc. Now-a-days, there being no upper limit, retired personnel appointed as arbitrators are charging a whopping Rs. 5,000/- to Rs. 10,000/- per each hearing of 2 hour duration. Some of them are getting for this part time work, an income far exceeding the salary and perks they would have received while in regular employment. An arbitrator should not take up more than two arbitration matters concurrently at any point of time. Some arbitrators are taking up too many cases at a time in their eagerness to earn more money. Such arbitrators are often finding it difficult to do justice to their job. If any arbitrator is found to be corrupt, he/she should be debarred from acting as an arbitrator for a minimum of two years, and for a life time if his/her offence is very serious. Such action could be taken by a forum like the Indian Society of Arbitrators on the basis of charges made against them and the evidence produced.

With regard to the procedure, the parties should be required to submit their cases in writing as briefly as possible enclosing therewith only the relevant copies of the records in the very first sitting. Each of the parties should be required to give their replies to the plaint of the other within a fortnight. In the third hearing which should be held within one month from the date of the 2nd hearing, the arbitrator should give a list of his/her queries for clarification, after reading the cases put forth by the parties. He/she should specify that each party should present its case/give clarifications orally within a duration of 10 hours spread over four sittings. Accordingly, the four sittings for each party may be given at intervals of one week and each sitting lasting for 2 to 3 hours. Within a fortnight after the last hearing, the award should be given by the arbitrator. The objection for limiting the time for presentation of case/arguments can be scotched by pointing out that even the epic Mahabharata can be narrated in one day, if the narrator is thorough with his subject and refrains from straying from the subject. Therefore, if the parties are thorough with their cases, they would be able to present their cases quite well within the specified time limit.

However, this procedure can be lengthened to the

maximum time limit of one year depending on the seriousness of the case, volume of papers to be perused and other extraordinary circumstances. Once the award is given, obtaining a rule of court should be more or less like a formality. The court should not take more than a fortnight for this purpose, unless very serious lapses on the part of the arbitrator are brought to its notice.

At present an arbitrator is not accountable to any one. Some of them are resorting to corrupt practices to make money by giving awards favouring one of the parties. This is happening particularly in case of private parties against Government Departments/Organisations. Some of the corrupt Government officials connive with the private companies in getting a favourable award for the latter. If an arbitrator drops out without giving an award, he/she should be required to pay back 50% of the fee received by him/her and also be debarred from acting as an arbitrator for two years, at least.

The replacement of a sole arbitrator or one or more of the arbitrators in a multi number tribunal as and when a vacancy arises should be simple and easy. For instance, if an arbitrator appointed by one of the parties resigns, the party should have the power to appoint another person to fill up the vacancy without need for getting consent of the other party and the other arbitrator/arbitrators. There should not be any need to approach a court for this purpose.

Some of the arbitrators are giving awards in a frivolous manner, either because of monetary consideration or due to insufficient effort to study and understand the case referred to them. Some of them are having prejudices against some professions. In order to make the arbitrators conscious of their responsibility, they should be required to take an oath in the name of God or by affirmation that they would conduct the proceedings impartially and try their best to understand the case properly and to give an unbiased and equitable award. If they are known for their fairmindedness, the parties may even agree for a mediation by the arbitrators for reaching a settlement during the course of arbitration. The parties should refrain from keeping the arbitrators under perpetual threat of being accused of misconduct.

Finally, it is perhaps good for the arbitrators to remember Napolean's saying that 'There is nothing more immoral than to occupy a place you cannot fill.' Therefore, they should agree to arbitrate only in such disputes for which they sincerely feel they are competent.

17

Education and Examinations

The goals of evolving an ideal education system and its effective implementation have yet to be achieved. No doubt, many steps have already been taken in this direction, since the attainment of Independence. But they are far too inadequate and some of them are not in the right direction.

The number of schools and colleges has increased manifold, although they are still not enough to cater to the full requirement. The syllabi and curriculum in the schools and colleges have been updated and changed from time to time. For instance, in good old days, one had to complete the eleventh class known as S.S.L.C. before entering a college. For seeking admission into a four year degree course in engineering one had to complete "intermediate" of two years duration in a college. Thus, one had to be in a college for six years for getting a B.E. or an equivalent degree after the eleventh class. But now, one has to study for six years after the 10th class only for getting a B.E. Degree. Thus, in the present system, a student can get some of his/her degrees in a duration that is one year less than that was required in olden days.

Subjects like History and Geography which were being taught as separate subjects have now been clubbed into one subject known as Social Sciences. Undoubtedly, many of these changes have improved the quality of education in tune with the alround advancement in the world.

The old detention system in schools was resulting in the blockage of several seats in each class which otherwise would have been available to students seeking new admissions. Happily, now this system has been more or less dispensed with, in the schools. The authorities must have realised that the difference between a student passing with 35% marks and another failing with 34% marks is very little. This has also come to the rescue of such students who are good in many subjects but are too weak in one or two subjects.

While the above changes are quite laudable and have achieved the desired results to a large extent, there is still a vast scope to bring about many more improvements. For any educational system to become successful, the following are the most important factors.

(1) Teachers dedicated to their profession with sufficient knowledge and aptitude for teaching.

(2) Students who are interested in the subjects that they choose for their studies and

(3) The infrastructure like buildings for schools and colleges, text books, libraries, laboratories, other equipment, funds for salaries, and general administration etc.

In the world in general and in our country in particular, a majority of the people are not seeking jobs or pursuing professions in the areas of their aptitude. Their preference is depending on what they consider as lucrative jobs or professions. For instance, one may be interested in studying history. But he tries to get admission into an engineering college or a medical college either due to pressure from his elders or because of his own perception of his future prospects. Perhaps, most of such students could give an average performance in such areas of their choice. But, surely they could give much better performance in the areas in which they have got an aptitude.

There was a time when one was choosing the teaching profession almost as a last resort, as the salaries and promotional opportunities were limited. Those with aptitude for teaching were preferring jobs in other areas because of the advantages like better emoluments, higher perks, status and power.

In the recent times, the salaries, perks and career advancement opportunities have increased considerably for teachers in the educational institutions barring a few exceptions. This has resulted in a phenomenal increase in the number of aspirants to fill these posts. But, many of them are choosing the profession not so much because of their liking for the profession as for the opportunities it provides in the advancement of their careers. The administration and the educationists should give a thought to this aspect while formulating their plans for imparting education to the students, if they want to make full use of the potential of the student community for the benefit of the country and the world. This will become possible only when the disparities in the salaries and perks for the people employed in various departments are reduced and reasonable employment opportunities are provided to all the educated youth according to their qualifications.

Our objective to provide free and compulsory education to all the children upto the age of 14 years remains a dream yet to be translated into a reality. This is no doubt a difficult - nay- a stupendous task. But it is not impossible to achieve in a period of 10 to 15 years, if there is a will and determination. As a first step, the Government should either directly or through voluntary and private organisations set up a school in every village and impart basic education to the children.

There need not be pucca buildings for this purpose immediately. These schools should function at the timings convenient to the children, preferably in the evenings, as many of them attend to their work in the fields during the day time. Like the incentives offered to the doctors and the people in promoting/implementing the family planning programme, teachers, educated youth, and retired persons should be given incentives to go to the nearby villages and teach the children during summer vacations. Every industry and business house should be asked to undertake the work of educating the children in one to 20 villages depending on the size of the industry/business house.

One more aspect in the present day educational system which requires a thorough review is the system of public examinations for the 10th and 12th class. It is widely believed that the present form of examinations is the best, if not the only way to ascertain the knowledge of the students. But, in reality, this is neither efficient nor essential.

Holding of the examinations in the present form is costing a lot of money and causing needless hardship and uncertainty to the students. Now and then, re-examinations are being held as a result of prevalance of turbulent conditions and/or leakage of question papers. Sometimes, the question papers are set, by including questions not covered by the syllabus, giving the impression that the person who set the papers is either ignorant of the syllabus or intending to show off his own knowledge. After every examination, there is a hue and cry from the students and their parents on this score forcing the Central Board of Secondary Education to resort to moderation/ weightage etc in the evaluation of the answer books. The system of multiple set question papers has left the students to depend on their luck, as in the same examinations, some are getting easy questions and the others difficult questions. Elaborate arrangements deploying armed police at the examination centres are made, ostensibly to prevent malpractices like copying by the students. This gives the impression that the students would resort to unfair means, if such strict vigilance and security measures are not applied. Does this mean that the examinations held in the schools for the other classes without these security measures are not to be given credence?

The answer books of the students of one school are sent to the teachers of a different school for evaluation. There are instances — though admittedly they are not too many-of some brilliant students getting lower ranks than less intelligent students. This could be because of many reasons, like the following:

1. Some students would have expected the questions correctly and prepared well to answer them.

2. Some students might have resorted to cheating, inspite of the presence of the invigilators.

3. The nature of the evaluators and their moods.

4. Mixing up of the registered numbers.

5. Mistakes in totalling of the marks.

All these anomalies can be eliminated if an alternative system of evaluation as described below is adopted.

It is an undeniable fact that the class teachers are the best judges of the calibre, performance and knowledge of their students as they observe them through-out the academic year. Therefore let each school conduct the examinations for the 10th and 12th classes also within their school premises. Based on their marks in that examination as well as their performance through-out the year, the students should be given ratings in their certificates as x/y where x is the rank and y is the total number of students in the class in that school. Suppose, some one has performed well through-out the year but has failed to appear for the annual examinations due to illness or some other unavoidable circumstances, he should still be declared to have passed, of course by reducing his rating by a few points. The certificate should contain the rank as stated above, the percentage of his attendence in the class, grading of his performance through-out the year, the subjects in which he has an aptitude and the subjects in which he is particularly weak.

One can point out that the teachers' likes and dislikes may deprive some students of a fair deal and that this system does not give the students their rankings on a state wide basis. As for the former, it is not as serious as the defects of the present system. More over, individual cases of favouritism/victimisation can be brought to the attention of the principal or a committee of teachers for redressal.

Regarding the state wise ranking, the present system is unreasonable as there is no uniformity in teaching in all schools and the evaluation of all the answer books. The states in our country are not of equal size. It is not fair therefore to compare the first rank student of a large state with that of a small state. Moreover, entrance examinations or interviews are being held for admission into any course after the 12th class or for recruitment for any jobs. As such, ranking on a state wide basis are not called for.

18

Medium of Instruction

The question of the medium of instruction for collegiate education is one of the many issues of the present day which are being distorted and whose importance exaggerated quite out of proportion. One has to analyse the facts relating to this question impassionately to have a clear understanding as to how much more serious this is made to appear than actually it is.

At the outset, one has to understand how poor the standard of a vast majority of students is in English although they study with English as their medium of instruction in colleges. It is no exaggeration that many graduates do not know even how to write an application for an appointment or for leave. Apart from this, it has to be understood that there is no relation between a man's knowledge in English, and his proficiency in any subject or work.

The antagonists to the policy of introducing Tamil as the medium of instruction in colleges in Tamil Nadu are advancing the following argument while pleading for the status quo.

1. It is difficult to teach the various subjects, especially in engineering, technology and medicine in Tamil as all the texts are available in English only. Translation of these texts into Tamil is difficult if not impossible as equivalent terms for the

English technical terms are not available. It is difficult for any one to keep abreast of the latest advances in the technical fields as most of the research reports etc. are published in English, the world over.

2. It is not possible for the students studying with Tamil as the medium of instruction to compete for the All India Services and they will be handicapped in seeking employment in other States as they will lack adequate knowledge in English.

The above arguments, although catchy and seemingly sound are unrelated to the facts.

It is an undeniable fact that any student in our country can learn any subject better if it is taught in his or her mother tongue than if it is taught in English language. Here, it is not attempted to under-rate the status or importance of English language. Nor is it intended to dispute the richness of the language, its extreme capability for clear and accurate expression and its wide-spread popularity in many countries because of historical reasons.

It is only tried to impress the difficulty experienced by most people in understanding the language clearly when it is used as medium of instruction in colleges, at any rate, in the first few years after their admission in college. The translation of the English text books into Tamil is though difficult, not an impossible task. Great epics like Mahabharata and Ramayana written originaly in Sanskrit have been translated into Tamil and other important languages in the country. There is no need for finding equivalent terms in these languages for their corresponding English terms. Many of the words in English could be retained as they are in Tamil language. In many European countries, Latin American countries and in some Asian and African countries they are using their own national/ local languages as their medium of instruction. Countries like Japan, Germany and Russia do not feel in anyway handicapped by using their languages in the colleges.

On the other hand, they are not only keeping pace with the modern technological developments but also they have contributed much to the treasure of literature in English in the various science subjects. Once, great research work is reported in Tamil or any other language even foreign people will try to learn that language. There are many students presently who know the subject well but find it very difficult to write or explain the same in English. Thus it could be seen that the change of medium of instruction to Tamil is going to be greatly beneficial to the students.

Regarding the second point in the above argument; it has to be pointed out that English language is not altogether given up in the studies in colleges. It will still continue to be one of the subjects to be taught in the institutions. As such, those interested in learning English well will still have ample scope to do so.

Regarding the plea that the change of medium of instruction will adversely affect the chances of the students of non-Hindi states in the All India Services examinations, it has to be pointed out that there is a proposal to conduct the U.P.S.C. examinations in all regional languages and hence this difficulty will not exist. Those seeking employment in other States must, of course learn the language of that State.

The bulk of the college students will take up jobs within their states only. All of them could very well manage even if they study in colleges with their regional language as the medium of instruction. Comparatively a smaller percentage of students seek jobs in the Central Government or other States. Those people should learn a language of the State where they take up their profession. Such people should make a special study in English to improve their knowledge of that language. But it is unjustified to compel a vast majority of students to study in English for the sake of the convenience of a small percentage of students and thereby make it difficult for them to understand the subjects. Learning an additional language or improving one's standard in English by intensive study may be considered as very difficult at the first glance. But let us take the example of those seeking scholarships for higher studies in Russia, Germany, France, Japan etc. It is generally stipulated that for eligibility to get these scholarships, the candidates should have a sound knowledge of the language of the country where they intend to carry out their higher studies. The students are all learning these languages without too much difficulty. In that way any other Indian language or English could be learnt well within a reasonable time. To facilitate this, in Universities special intensive courses may be introduced to give a thorough knowledge of any language to a student who wishes to learn a language. This will be also useful for students of one state to study in the Universities located in another state.

However much we may learn English, our accent is never the same as the Englishman's. Very few of the educated could express themselves very clearly in English. With the same effort made to learn one's mother tongue a student will succeed in acquiring a much more thorough mastery over that language. To quote an Englishman, Sir Winston Churchill writes in his autobiography that the English students must learn english well. A knowledge of any other language like Latin and Greek may be of great additional advantage. But if the study of English is neglected while acquiring knowledge in Latin or Greek, the students would stand to a great disadvantage. What he stated for English students, applies with equal relevance to students in Tamil Nadu.

The question of medium of instruction should be treated in its proper academic light and tackled in a suitable way bearing in mind as to what might be the best for the great majority of students. This should never be treated as a political problem. Passions should not be roused with the intention of fishing in troubled waters. The only consideration in taking any decision should be that which is likely to be most beneficial to the students.

Note: This article was written in 1971. The word "Tamil" may be replaced by the words "regional language" in this article.

19

Women : Their Problems - Suggested Remedies

It is a well known fact that women are faced with many problems in society. By nature too, they have inherited certain weaknesses and dis-advantages, physically. In general, they are dependant on men for their protection, social position and livelihood. Therefore, it is not surprising that many of them are exploited, taken for granted, suppressed and subjected to harsh restrictions, cruel rules and unreasonable customs.

In the recent times, women have been freed from some of these shackles. Quite a few of them are now well educated and some of them are giving a very good account of themselves in politics, administration, judiciary, art, science and technology, business and many more fields. Indira Gandhi, Madam Curie, Jane Austin, Mother Teresa and many more great ladies have achieved greatness and covered themselves with glory for their outstanding work in their respective fields. Indeed, they are in no way less than the great men of their times in their respective fields. Such ladies have illuminated the seemingly ever dark horizon for women with bright flashes of light and filled their hearts with a hope that in the not too distant a future, they could play their role in society on more or less equal terms with men.

There are many women's organisations which are fighting

ceaselessly for women's rights and "liberation". Many men also say that they have been striving to remove the social disadvantages being suffered by women. But, at best, their efforts are achieving marginal results only. The reasons for this are lack of sincerity in some cases and failure to identify clear cut goals in most cases. Despite their pretentions of sympathy for women's causes and their upliftment, men are revealing their intolerance of women exercising power in public life. Their hatred for assertive women with a mind of their own is so great that they would not hesitate to adopt any means - fair or foul - to dislodge them from their positions and to discredit them.

Till a few decades ago, women were not having voting rights in many countries. Women were not allowed to have their own bank accounts. They could not inherit their parents' property along with their brothers. Even today, in a few countries, women are denied these rights. In some societies, while men can divorce their wives, women do not enjoy the right to divorce their husbands. Women are required to wear 'burquas' or veils to cover their faces whereas men have no such restrictions. Widows are required to follow certain norms in dress and their get-up whereby they could be recognised as widows from their appearance. Men are allowed to marry after the death of their wives. But women are looked down upon by the society if they marry again after the death of their husbands. With the dowry system assuming the form of a terrible monster in society, people are dreading the prospect of begetting a female child. With the advance in the medical sciences, some parents are detecting the sex of the child in the womb and are resorting to abortion if it happens to be a female. Perhaps, these instances are not so many as it is made to look like in the articles in the newspapers and magazines. Nevertheless, this trend itself is an alarming one and needs to be curbed.

Some of these problems can be solved by legislation and the rest through social organisations. For improving the women's lot and in order to give them their rightful place in society, the following legislations may be enacted.

(1) The women voters constitute nearly 50% of the total electorate in our country. Therefore, let it be laid down that 50% of the seats in all the legislatures are reserved for women. Here, it is not suggested that each political party should put up women candidates for 50% of the seats to be contested by it. In that case, the actual numbers of women elected may not necessarily constitute 50 % of the strength of the legislature, as women candidates of one party may be pitted against men candidates of other parties. What is proposed is that one man and one woman should be elected from each constituency for Lok Sabha and State Vidhan Sabhas. If the number of seats in these legislatures have to be kept at the present level only, the constituencies may be demarcated afresh and enlarged by clubbing two adjoining constituencies. Promises of political parties that 30% of seats will be reserved for women are like throwing crumbs to satisfy them. Once, politically they become strong, they will be able to solve many of their problems more easily by themselves.

(2) Women should have equal rights with men for the inheritence of their parents'/ancestral property. This will help in reducing the menace of the dowry system to a large extent.

Here, it may be interesting to go into the probable origin of the dowry system in our society. For a young couple to set up their own home after marriage, they need several things for which they might not be having the resources to procure. Therefore, the parents or the brothers of the bride used to give all the house-hold articles like utensils, cot, bed, a little jewellery and or money as she would not have any right to inherit their property. The bride groom was supposed to inherit a share in his father's property and was expected to be the breadwinner by doing work/business somewhere. There is also a practice of the guests at the marriage ceremony to give gifts in the form of house hold articles or money to the newly married couple. These gifts are like interest-free loans given to the couple in order to give a helping hand in running their house hold in the initial stages after their marriage, until they are well settled to stand on their own legs. The prevelant custom is to make a note of the cash and other gifts given by the relations and friends and to give them back in the form of gifts equal in value whenever functions are held in their houses. This is like repaying the loan in instalments. But, the system which was meant to be beneficial to the society has come to be abused and exploited so much that it has taken the shape of an ugly and terrible social evil.

(3) Cases of eve-teasing and rape should be dealt with by a person of the locality within an area covered by the jurisdiction of each police station. Such a person could be appointed by the District Court or the High Court for a period of 3 years and designated as a Society Judge. These persons need not necessarily have a law degree or a legal background. They should be elderly persons with a record of unimpeachable personal character. Their remuneration should be fixed on a case to case basis or as a nominal monthly honorarium. The hearings can be held either at the person's residence or in the local police station premises. The powers of the Society Judges should be spelt out. This system would ensure that the guilty persons are punished without delay. Further, the work load on the Judiciary will be reduced to some extent. The women will find it much easier to approach a local Society Judge for speedy justice than to approach the Judiciary/Courts where the procedures are too elaborate, delays are enormous and the expenses are prohibitive.

Some of the problems which can be tackled by social organisations are mentioned below. Only a reformer of the calibre of Raja Ram Mohan Roy could bring about an end to the cruel and abnoxious practice of "Sati". Legislation could be effective only after the social awakening was created by him.

(1) In the same way, widow remarriages may be allowed by law. But, in practice, they would become prevelant and socially acceptable only when social organisations bring about the necessary change in the out-look and thinking in the society.

(2) The burqua system in the society also appears to be

quite an oppressive custom. This custom must have originated from a man's thinking that a woman is his possession and the exposure of her face to other men could lead to arousal of evil desires in their minds. It is to be examined how far this is valid in the modern society.j

In their zest for giving equal rights to women, people should not lose sight of the many good things in the age old traditions in each society. For instance, a woman is expected to do certain household jobs like cooking, washing and housekeeping in an average middle class family. Though she appears to play a subordinate role to her hushand, she is often treated with love and esteem. In most of the families, the women willingly subject themselves to the gentle hegemony of their husbands. But for minor incidents of quarrels or differences, the women are by and large happy with their lives with their husbands. In the name of giving equality, the happy balance of harmony and concern for mutual welfare should not be upset. For, men and women are expected to play their respective roles which are complementary to one another. Both should not try to play the same role or each other's role. This could prove to be detrimental to both and to the society, in general.

Here, it should be noted that neither all men are the exploiters nor all women, the exploited. There are countless cases of women tormenting men folk also. Some of them have struck terror in the hearts of men as dacoits, conspirators, despots etc. There are examples of women acquiring a notoriety as criminals and evil doers even from our Puranic age. But, as fair sex, women should be treated with chivalry and consideration in spite of minor lapses on their part. In turn, for the privileges and protection that they expect from men, women should be prepared to stop clamouring for equality in all respects. Indeed, women should be a little more than equal to men in some areas while being a little less than equal in some other areas.

Both the Government and the social organisations should do their best in giving quick relief to the victims of the brutalities of men. The perpetrators of crimes like rape on women should be given a deterrant punishment in addition to confiscation of a part of their properties. Those who have no property should be made to pay a proportion of their earnings for the rest of their lives or for a fixed period of about 5 to 10 years. These properties and moneys should be kept in a Trust from which the victims should be provided with the needful succour. The society should treat the victims of rape more kindly. They should not be attached with a stigma.

In case a woman finds it impossible to live with her husband due to incompatibility, harassment from her husband or in-laws, frequent quarrels resulting in violence, it should be made possible for her to get separated from her husband without having to go through the court procedures for obtaining a divorce. Many women are too shy or afraid of the publicity to go to court. This procedure is in vogue in certain castes and is quite commonly followed in the rural areas in our country. The caste heads in the locality grant such divorces.

It is also high time that the restrictions on women pursuing studies in the Vedas etc. are removed. When women are excelling in every branch of learning, it sounds absurd to put such restraints on them, any longer.

One more vexed problem faced by some unfortunate women is the branding of their children as illegitimate. This causes even greater harm to and psychological stress on such children for no fault of theirs.

The children of such couples who have lived together declaring themselves as man and wife should be accepted as legitimate, irrespective of whether the couples are really married or not. It may also be stipulated that if a man signs on the birth certificate/school certificate or any other document of this nature, as the father of a child, that child should be recognised in law and society as his legitimate child.

20

Incompatibility of Caste System in Modern Society

Caste system is perhaps a unique feature of the Hindu society. Castes—at any rate, as they are understood in the Hindu society—are not to be found among the people of other religions.

It is generally agreed that the caste came into being, based on the professions allocated to or carried on by different groups or sections of the people. Broadly, the people were classified into four main castes or sects known as Brahmans, Kshatriyas, Vysyas and Sudras. The professions allocated to these castes respectively were priesthood, rulership, business and cultivation of lands.

Functions of Different Sects

Because the Brahmans were allocated the selfless and noble work of priesthood and teachership they were generally acclaimed as of high caste deserving veneration of all the people. They were expected to spend their time in an unostentatious and ascetic manner.

The Brahmans were required to read all the scriptures and to disseminate scriptural knowledge to their disciples. They were to lead a pious life, setting an example in good conduct to others. They were expected to perform all religious rituals for the people and were to be "Purohitas" meaning, the well-wishers of the community.

The duties laid down for Kshatriyas were rulership and defence of the country. They were expected to be physically very strong, courageous by nature, upright in dispensation of justice and ready to lay down their lives cheerfully in the defence of the country. They were to be the guardians of the country in peace time and the saviours in war time.

The Vysyas had business, as their share of the work. All the trade and commerce were to be their province. The purchase of grain in villages where it is produced, the sale of grain, spices, clothes, jewels, import and export of goods etc. were completely entrusted to that community.

Finally, the Sudras were entrusted with the cultivation of lands for producing food grains, vegetables etc. As time passed more professions like, weaving clothes, blacksmithy, sculpture had also to be taken up by sub-sections of the Sudras. Thus the Sudras were expected to be skilled in various professions like tilling the land, blacksmithy, goldsmithy, weaving, sculpture, washing clothes etc. The people engaged in each of these professions formed a caste of their own.

Thus there are greater number of castes among the sect of Sudras as compared to the number of subsects among the remaining three divisions namely, brahmans, kshatriyas and vysyas. The Sudras were generally very simple, hardworking, quiet-going, unsophisticated by virtue of the nature of their work.

Order of Importance

Although the various castes might, quite likely, have been more or less equal at the time of their origination, since the division was more for convenience and of functional nature, in due course, the order of importance or superiority of the castes was laid down and accepted as below.

The Brahmans being entrusted with such materially unprofitable and unrewarding work as acquisition of knowledge and rendering service to the community by spreading the knowledge among people and performing rituals believed to be beneficial to the community, were held in high respect and were considered as of the highest caste. They were believed to have a sort of effulgence, radiance and brightness in their faces and other features of the body.

Because of the military power in their hands, the Kshatriyas came to be hailed as of the second highest caste. It was generally believed that the Vysyas were very shrewd in bargaining and cunning by nature having always the aim of making the maximum profit. By virtue of their money and influence resulting from their profitable profession of business, they could occupy the third place in the order of superiority among the castes. The Sudras were thus relegated to the fourth place.

Inherent Defects

This system might have worked smoothly and harmoniously in the initial stages. But later on, the inherent defects of this system came to the surface. Many of the Brahmans being worshipped as the gods on the earth (Bhoosuras) became arrogant.

A large number of the Kshatriyas regarded as the champions of the defence of the country became powerdrunk and tended to be highhanded. Most of the Vysyas were amassing wealth and were using all their cunning and stealth in entrenching themselves in their lucrative profession and to monopolise the same.

Sudras, although not wholly dissatisfied with their lot, were beginning to feel their inferior status. Marriages, social intercourse, relationship etc. among the people were restricted to their respective castes. The tendency to perpetuate their privileges and to enhance their rights and power grew stronger among the various castes.

It was considered an unpardonable offence for any one other than Brahmans to read Vedas and other religious scriptures. Education for other castes was generally discouraged. In the name of scriptures, it was attempted to put the Brahmans on an entirely different and higher footing.

For instance, it is generally laid down that taking the life of a human being is a heinous sin. But taking the life of a brahman known as "brahma hatya" is said to be many times more sinful. This evidently shows the bias in the scripture which must be the result of the brahmans' wish for better protection.

Similarly when something was to be given as alms for acquiring merit and heavenly blessings, it was stipulated that such gifts were to be made to suitable Brahmans. In the same fashion, the Kshatriya rulers framed regulations which were best suited to their autocratic disposition. In course of time, the barriers between the various castes became much stronger and almost insurmountable.

Many Brahmans were taking advantage of the ignorance of the people of other castes for their own benefit. Some of them were misusing their privileged positions for acquiring wealth and power through dishonest means. They were becoming more and more addicted to vices and were craving for a life of ease and comfort. All their sins were explained away by citing the scriptural immunity from punishment available to them.

In the modern age, great changes have taken place in the social and economic spheres. Science and technology have shaken the structure of society. Many professions that could not have been imagined of at the time of the origination of caste system have now sprung up.

If engineering profession in its present form had been existing at that time, surely there would have been a separate caste or a subsect for the people engaged in that profession. If aeroplanes had been there, then all the pilots would have been included in a separate caste.

Loosening of Barriers

In the present day India, many Brahmans can be seen in possession of lands and engaging themselves in cultivation. For the Kshatriyas, there are no kingdoms to rule. Today people from all sects are engaged in politics and administration of the country. Business is no longer the exclusive privilege and monopoly of Vysyas. People of all castes are carrying on business with the same degree of skill and talent.

Sudras have also cut across their tradition-bound barriers and many are taking up professions like teaching, administration, business etc. Thus it can be seen that the castes as visualised originally have no real meaning in the present day society. Indeed they have lost all their significance, validity and relevance.

In spite of all the above facts being a common knowledge, and in spite of constant, though feeble, efforts of the Government and several progressive social reformers, the caste system is firmly entrenched and there are many who assiduously and dogmatically cling to it. Many people try to favour and help the people of their caste although no relationship exists between them.

Instinctive Affinity

A Brahman in Tamilnadu may have more differences in the mode of dress, method of worship, habits of diet and in social customs with a Brahman from Orissa or Bengal than with people of other castes within the State. Yet, instinctively, he feels an affinity for the person belonging to his sect, despite the differences and distance. Likewise, the Kshatriyas of one State harbour fellow feeling for those of another State even if there is a gulf of difference betwen them in their manners, tempermanent, habits and culture. The Brahmans of Tamilnadu, Andhra, etc. may claim credit for being vegetarian. But those of Orissa and Bengal do not consider it improper to eat fish and mutton.

Certainly, vegetarianism alone could not make a person superior to others and worthy of respect, whatever be its virtues. If it could, the numerous people among the other castes who remain strict vegetarians either out of a real dislike for non-vegetarian food or because of a resolve taken by them would also deserve the same respect from others.

Gross Ignorance

There are among Brahmans many who are very ignorant, ill-educated, shabby and impious. Many still exploit the accident of their birth as Brahmans for claiming superiority over others. The Brahmans do not have any special physical features that would distinguish them as being of that caste. Indeed, they are just like the people of other castes in their physical features.

Many staunch believers in the caste system do not even know the significance of a number of common Hindu festivals. Many admit their ignorance but would not shed their pride and give up their conceit. One "Purohit" in a famous temple explained the significance of the idol of Durga with the head of a buffalo under Her feet in the following way.

Durga fought an Asura for nine days without success. Finally on the tenth day, she came to the battle field with a buffalo as her "Vahanam" and vanquished the Asura. But any well informed Hindu knows the legend that Durga killed an Asura by name Mahishasura who could take the shape of a "Mahisha" meaning a buffalo.

The plan of some governments to appoint people of all castes as priests in the temples if they are properly qualified in the prescribed courses is being denouced mostly by hidebound, reactionary and other interested persons. The present state of the knowledge of the hereditary Brahman priests also justifies the Government plans in the matter of such recruitment. At least by this, priests having sound knowledge of the rituals to be performed could be chosen.

Professional Disintegration

Similarly the Kshatriyas, who also boast of their higher caste, have not been following their prescribed professions. How many of the Kshatriyas are ruling kingdoms? How many are serving in military for the defence of the country? Are not there many who are engaged in business and agriculture?

If the professions prescribed for the Kshatriyas are no

longer followed, why should the caste exist as such or why should they believe that they are still of the second highest caste? Can we call a short and ugly person or a lean and weak person or a timid and awkward person or a person having no self-respect a Kshatriya? There are all these types of people among Kshatriyas as among people of any other caste.

Indeed a school teacher has once jocularly remarked that the Kshatriyas of the old wielded their sword in the battle field and their descendants in the modern world are using knives and ladles in hotels, run by them. He was referring to the many Kshatriya hotels existing in Andhra Pradesh. If one delves deep into the superficial sarcasm, one could understand the truth of the observation which may be applicable to all castes.

A Shame on Society

Similarly, among Vysyas and Sudras there are all types of people, honest, dishonest; upright, crooked; learned, ignorant; physically very attractive, ugly; bold, cowardly, intelligent and dull. Some of them are as learned in puranas as any Brahman could wish himself to be. Some are showing their talent in the sphere of administration as well as any Kshatriya could do so.

If we pick a dozen people at random from a crowd, it would be difficult to identify their castes from their appearances. When the real state of affairs is such, will it not be wiser to deflate the importance of the caste system which has so many evils attending it? Because of the mutual jealousy, hatred, and suppression, the country's progress is being hampered. If the reading of the Vedas had not been prohibited for some castes, perhaps, they would have also contributed much to the enrichment of the scriptures. Similarly if the trades like weaving, blacksmithy, sculpture had been open for people of all castes, and were profitable,, the contribution of the people of the other castes would have been quite substantial.

In many high-caste families, it is taught that the people of lower castes are inferior, ignorant, shabby and not devout. But the above qualities depend on the family circumstances, environment, personal temperament rather than on caste.

There are many families among Sudras with high traditions, healthy habits, pious virtues and they are much better than many Brahmans. The plight of the Harijans or the so-called untouchables is a shame on Hindu society.

The highly enlightened, forward-looking and progressive people of all castes have never tried to claim superiority on account of their mere birth in a particular caste. They have preached equality of all the castes and they themselves have set an example in that respect. Great people like Nehru have never attached any importance to the caste.

There are several stories like that of Dharmavyadha illustrating that a man's virtues, and not his caste, alone would entitle him for respect. Great religious savants like Vivekananda have preached the above truth. But still the roots of this system are very firm. Whatever the outward slogans, all the political parties give due weight to the predominant castes of the various constituencies in the matter of selection of their candidates for an election.

Obduracy

One dogmatic person argued that Brahmans were being generally denied seats in Engineering and Medical colleges and they were being denied promotion and high jobs in the services. But when it was pointed out that in the colleges, reservation of seats is there only for economically backward castes to help them to come up to the level of the other castes and all the economically and educationally forward communiteis, including Brahmans are treated on par and on the basis of merit only, he would not agree.

This clearly shows the obduracy of mind and grim determination to be blind to the facts. There may be the tendency to victimise people on basis of caste but that is common to all castes. The reason for some Brahmans to be frustrated might be simple.

There was a time when education was almost the sole privilege of the Brahmans. They had been predominant in all institutions of learning by virtue of tradition. They were getting all scholastic honours and were considered meritorious. But when the advantages of education spread to many other castes, an element of competition entered the situation. And now the honours have to be shared with the students of the other castes.

Freedom of Belief

The purpose of writing this essay is certainly not to try to persuade people to give up tradition as such. By all means what is good in tradition must be tenaciously followed. If one finds a great deal of mental peace in worshipping a particular deity in a particular traditional manner one should certainly do it. But by doing so, if he claims to be superior than others, it has to be opposed tooth and nail and freedom of belief or disbelief and worship asserted.

There are many parties and organisations which fight the evils perpetrated by the caste system. Even a cursory glance at the things described above will amply justify the objectives of such organisations if not the methods adopted for achieving them. There are some arch reactionaries who suggest that the caste system, the religious communities etc. are a reality and hence they should be taken for granted and allowed to stay. It is like saying that the germs of cholera or other epidemics are real and hence should be allowed to take their toll and no attempt should be made to eradicate them.

A New Social Order

When the different castes are no longer pursuing the professions allotted to them originally, their existence becomes ridiculous. Any profitable profession, be it washing clothes, hair cutting, engineering, medicine, business, is sought after by people of all castes equally and arduously. The social customs, habits, cleanliness, virtues depend more on a man's family, surroundings and his own inherent qualities than on his caste.

The absence of any relationship between a man's intelligence, merit, worth, respectability, honesty, sincerity, suavity, bravery, farsightedness etc. and his caste is beyond doubt.

Hence it is time that a check is put on the divisive and harmful tendencies bred by the animosities arising from the caste system. While trying to achieve amity between people of various religious faiths, one should also devote one's energies to bring about good will, unity and harmony between the several castes of Hindu society.

The caste system, whatever good it might have done in the past, is now a dead weight on the society and certainly has outlived its utility. It will be worthwhile if all progressive people started a campaign highlighting the evils of the caste system and tried to propagate the necessity for a new social order in which the dignity of man and the concept of universal brotherhood will be upheld and observed in practice.

21

Housing-Problems of Tenants and Landlords

House is one of the prime needs of a family. Almost everyone desires to have a house of his own. Whatever be one's profession, he would have a sense of fulfilment if he could either construct or purchase a house for his family.

While rich people are living in palatial bungalows or luxury flats provided with all amenities, poor people are living in slums and jhuggis in miserable conditions. Some of the middle class people are owning houses which can be classified between the limits of "fairly good" to "a shade better than slum". But there are a large number of people in middle class and poor class who are not fortunate enough to have their own houses for various reasons like the rising prices and their inability to save and invest money.

Nearly 30 per cent of the urban population lives in rented accommodation of various categories as described above, depending on their financial capacity and living standards. Some of these rented houses are self contained and independant. However, the others are too small and lacking in privacy. Many of them are provided with common toilets, verandahs, sit-outs, electricity meters etc. The reason for this is that the houses constructed for one family are being partitioned into smaller portions and given on rent by the landlords. Usually, the landlord retains one portion for his own family. The tenants living in such portions of the houses experience a lot of problems daily. Use of common facilities as described above causes sometimes quarrels and quite often insanitary conditions.

The rents of the houses in cities like New Delhi are very high. If the tenant is a salaried employee, a good portion of his salary and allowances goes towards the payment of the rent of his house. The rent for a two bed room flat in South Delhi, for instance, ranges between a whopping Rs. 5,000/- and Rs. 7000/- per month (as existing in 1995) depending on its location and get-up. If the tenant happens to have at his disposal his own or his employer's car, he is required to park it on the road side only, in spite of paying such a high rent. Most of the private rented houses/flats are not provided with garages or parking places. Only some colonies like the DDA housing complexes in Delhi are provided with some parking space. Usually, the landlords are increasing the rents at least by 10 per cent every year. They also charge extra towards the cost of maintenance of a booster pump etc. The tenants are also required to pay an advance of 3 to 6 months rent as a security. The landlords do not bother even to get the routine maintenance work like painting and white washing done periodically in these houses. If the landlord happens to be living in the same premises he would often regulate the water supply, electric power and the movements of the tenants.

Of course, there are some cases of the tenants holding the landlords for ransom. Some of them are paying a paltry sum as the rent which might have been fixed 15 to 20 years ago. They are like a thorn in the flesh of the landlords. They are usually surly and rude and are prepared to use muscle power, if need be. Some other tenants in this category are big companies or influential and rich people and they take the legal recourse to keep the houses under their occupation at the absurdly low rents fixed several decades ago. The media is generally highlighting the travails of such landlords only. But, there are, perhaps many more cases of the tenants being harassed by the landlords.

Many of these tenants are the people who are dependant on their jobs in Government or private companies. They come from either a rural area or some other towns. Some of them do not know how long they would have to stay in the city. For, they might be working on a temporary basis or they might be transferred to another place by their employers. At the time of vacating the houses, they usually face a lot of problem in getting a refund of their security deposit.

Some people who happen to be in one city for a fairly long time would naturally think of buying or constructing a house for themselves. But their desires usually end up as day dreams only because of the following reasons:

(1) The land prices are galloping by leaps and bounds. This increase is usually manipulated by the real estate dealers. The circulation of black money is giving a stimulus to such manipulation.

(2) Some people are doing business by booking houses in certain colonies like the DDA housing complexes in Delhi and selling them at three to four times their purchase price after their allotment. For instance, people are demanding around Rs.8 lakhs for selling houses purchased by them at Rs. 2 lakhs hardly one year before.

(3) An honest employee in Government or private companies can hardly hope to save that much money even by the time he retires.

Government is often promising to give its attention to the housing problems of the people. But the results so far are not at all satisfactory. If the Government is really sincere, the following measures could be taken in order to relieve the people of this grave problem.

(1) Fix a limit on the profit one can make on the sale of land. For instance, if a person has purchased a house plot at Rs. 100/- per sq. yard, he/she should not sell the same land at more than Rs. 110/- per sq. yard at the end of one year. If he/she wants to sell it within one year, the price should be proportionately reduced. There are several instances of some

rich people in cities like Madras having minted money in the past 20 years by selling at exhorbitant prices the land on the outskirts of the city which they acquired at a throw away price more than 50 years ago. The profit should be limited to 10% per year on the initial investment in all the property deals.

(2) Real estate agents and property development companies should be asked to follow strict norms with regard to cost of land and profit there on as per the stipulation in (1) above. If any development work has been done like construction of drains, roads, laying water pipes and electric lines, the cost of it with 10 per cent profit thereon may be distributed on a proportional basis on the land cost.

(3) Anyone who has been allotted a house in a colony like the DDA housing complex should not sell his house for at least one year after its allotment. From then onwards, the house could be sold at his purchase price plus 10 per cent profit per annum only.

(4) As far as possible, one person should not be allowed to own more than one house plot in a city. He could construct one or more flats in this plot. This measure will reduce the demand on the prime land and thereby the price will come down. A rich man who could afford to have two houses in a city can as well own one house in his plot and take another on rent, if he really needs two houses.

(5) The rent of a house should be fixed at a specified rate per sq. m. of the plinth area in a "base year" in each locality of a city. The increase in the rent from the "base year" shall be at 5 per cent per annum only.

(6) The security deposit shall not be more than the amount equal to two months' rent.

(7) The tenant shall be required to give a notice of 2 months before vacating the house. He shall be permitted to adjust the security against the rent for the last two months.

(8) The tenant should not be penalised for normal wear and tear which is bound to happen in any house due to its occupation for a certain period.

(9) The tenant should get the repairs done at his own cost, if any damage is caused to the house due to his/her family's carelessness.

(10) The land lord should be required to give 6 months notice to the tenant, if he wants the house to be vacated.

(11) In each municipal ward, 10 retired officers/reputed persons should be nominated by the Government to act as arbitrators to resolve the disputes between land lords and tenants. They should be asked to resolve any dispute within two weeks and holding not more than 2 hearings. The verdict of the arbitrators shall be accepted without demur. If it is proved that any arbitrator is corrupt and has given a decision deliberately favouring one party, he should be debarred from being an arbitrator once for all. His remuneration should be nominal. Preferably, it should be between Rs. 250/- and Rs. 500/- per each dispute depending on the value of property. An arbitrator shall not deal with more than 10 cases in a month.

(12) Forcible eviction shall not be resorted to except under the orders of an arbitrator and in presence of a police official. Before such eviction, the tenant should be given a notice of 2 months about such an intended action.

It is reported that many houses allotted by Government to people like Ministers, MPs and high officials are not being vacated by the tenants even after they lose their eligibility to occupy them. Government must take firm action in such cases to create confidence in the minds of the people that the Government is not discriminatory.

(13) If the rule (12) above is violated and the land lord resorts to high handedness for evicting a tenant, such a land lord should be liable for prosecution.

(14) The reasons for such an eviction should be valid. They could be like any or all of the following.

(a) The tenant has failed to pay the rent for 2 months at a stretch.

(b) The tenant has caused major damage to the house due

to his carelessness or rough use.

(c) The tenant is carrying on objectionale business in the house or causing intolerable nuisance to the neighbours.

(d) The tenant has refused to vacate the house even after the period of 6 months as per the notice of the land lord.

(15) Government should make it compulsory for the factories and companies to construct quarters/provide leased accommodation for their employees.

(16) Government should provide quarters/leased accommodation for its employees.

(17) Government should arrange to construct houses of different categories at suitable locations and sell them to those not owning a house already at cost price. The number of such houses should be determined on the basis of the current demand.

(18) Government should move out some of its offices from Delhi and other big cities to outskirts or nearby towns. This will reduce congestion in big cities and help developing smaller towns.

(19) The industries should also be spread out instead of allowing them to be concentrated in and around big cities only.

(20) There should be a standardised lease agreement incorporating the relevant conditions as stated above and it should be considered to be valid if it is notorised. The elaborate procedure to get the agreements registered should be dispensed with.

22

Problems of Common Customers in Banks and Financial Institutions

It is gratifying to note that the Nationalised Banks are advised to be responsive to the needs of the common customer. But most of the Banks are not observing this advice in letter and spirit. Indeed, it is high time that the ordinary customer is given a fair deal. The banks and financial institutions should make him feel his importance in their business. Here stress is being laid on the "common" or "ordinary" customer because there is a lot of difference in treatment of the "common customer" and the "rich and privileged customer". The experiences of a few common customers are narrated below to illustrate how people like them suffer in their dealings with the banks and other financial institutions.

A person became a member of the ten year cumulative Time Deposit Scheme with the intention of saving a little in his income tax. As allowed in the terms of the scheme, he withdrew at the end of two years and again at the end of five years 50% of his deposits standing at his credit at those points of time. Later, when he closed his account at the end of the specified period, he got only a paltry sum. The reason for this was that the interest on the money that he had withdrawn from his own deposits was far higher than the interest paid to him on the amount at his credit. He wondered whether the scheme was really beneficial to him at all!

He learnt that a few years before the maturity of his CTD account, the rate of interest on loans (strictly speaking, withdrawals from the account holders' own deposits) was enhanced. Notwithstanding the fact that he started his contribution to the 10 year C.T.D. scheme much earlier, the recovery was made at the enhanced rate of interest. His pleas with the post office yielded no fruit. Furthermore, they told him that he could seek a legal remedy if he wanted to. But, the customer desisted from being provoked as his means were far from satisfactory.

A few years later, another customer joined a seven year Recurring deposit scheme in a Nationalised Bank. About two years later, the rate of interest on the Recurring deposits was increased. But the Bank Manager told him that the higher rate of interest was not applicable to his deposits as the recurring deposit scheme was like an agreement and the rate of interest remains constant during the currency of the scheme! He advised that if he wanted to avail of the higher rate of interest, he could close his R.D. at the end of three years and start a fresh R.D. Of course, by discontinuing the R.D. before its full seven year period, he would be losing some amount. That is, the Bank would not pay him even the full amount due for a normal three year R.D.

Once, a common man got an idea of starting a small scale industry. He made some studies, prepared a project report and enthusiastically submitted his application for a loan of about Rs. 10 lakhs in a Nationalised Bank. The Bank manager appreciated the project report and told that his application could be considered, if he could buy the land and also invest 20% of the project cost. In the face of these conditions his plans fizzled out.

Does not this rule give an edge to the rich class over the poorer sections of the intending entrepreneurs? If the Banks fear that the amount may not be repaid, if the enterpreneur does not invest 20%, why don't they fear about the repayment of the balance 80%? If the Banks are really so cautious, how is it that it is reported that a few of the so called big businessmen are getting away with playing frauds on the Banks?

Another person availed of a loan from the amount of premia paid towards his Life Insurance Policy. It was only about 50% of the amount paid by him already. At the time of the maturity of his policy the amount recovered towards the loan was more than twice the amount received by him as a loan, as it was calculated at an exhorbitant compound interest rate. No one would avail of a loan, if the living conditions are not hard and a pressing need does not arise. L.I.C. should bear in mind that the amount drawn as a loan was only a part of his own deposits and as such the least that they can do in a welfare state is to charge a nominal rate of simple interest, if they cannot allow outright withdrawl by a reducing the sum assured to that extent. It is the poorer sections (middle or lower middle classes included) that are greatly affected by this kind of unreasonable policy.

In another case, the P.F. Trust of a company issued a cheque to a person with the date of 10.8.1984 from Hyderabad. The cheque was received by him on 5.9.1984 at Raipur. He gave the cheque immediately to a Nationalised Bank for crediting the amount to his S.B. Account. The Bank collected the money and credited to his account on 30.9.1984. Thus, he was denied interest for the P.F amount for two months, i.e., August and September. As per the rules of the P.F. Trust, if any account is settled in the course of a month, the interest will be paid upto the end of the preceding month only. Similarly, if an account is transferred to the Trust, it will not pay interest for the month in which the transfer takes place.

In the case under reference, the concerned person wrote many letters and later personally argued with the members of the P.F. Trust saying that he should be paid interest at least for one month, if not for two months as the money was actually lying with the P.F. Trust until it was collected by his bank. Finally, the interest for one month was paid to him grudgingly. The Nationalised Bank never cared to tell the date of collection from the P.F. Trust. Strictly speaking, the P.F. Trust should have paid interest upto the date of collection of the amount by the Bank or it should have sent a demand draft for the amount with interest upto the date of the Demand Draft.

In another case, one person had given his pass book to the S.B.I. in a town in Madhya Pradesh with a request to get it transferred from their branch in a town in Andhra Pradesh. He had to go to the Bank several times to enquire whether the account was transferred. Finally, it was transferred after six weeks. But the concerned officer could not locate the pass book in a pile of books lying on his table in a haphazard fashion and therefore he issued a duplicate pass book, charging a fee for the same!

A few months later, he gave a refund order received from an income tax office in Andhra Pradesh and asked the Bank to collect the same and credit into his S.B. account. After one month, he went to the Bank to find out whether the money had been collected. The concerned officer told that it might take another one or two weeks for collection. But the money was not collected even after 2½ months. Then the customer pointed out that the "refund order bill" was valid for three months only and as such necessary steps should be taken for early collection. After another two weeks the officer told him that he had received a reply from the branch of the Bank in Andhra Pradesh saying that it had not received the bill. He advised the customer coolly to apply for a duplicate refund order from the income tax office!

Another person received a demand draft on a Nationalised Bank, at New Delhi from a town in Madhya Pradesh. When he presented it to the Bank for payment, he was asked to prove his identity. The person had shown his pass book of the S.B. Account in the branch which had issued the DD and also shown his driving licence on which his photograph with signature was affixed. But, the Branch Manager told that those documents were not enough. He told that he would accept a passport as a proof of his identity. The concerned person was not having his passport. A colleague of his who went along with him to the bank offered to sign as a witness. Even then, the bank officer did not budge. The person was in urgent need of money as he was transferred to Delhi just a few days earlier. Therefore, he threatened to report the matter to the higher officers of the Bank. Then, the concerned officer asked the person to tell the name of the Manager of the branch in which he stated he was having his S.B. A/C Luckily for him, he knew the name of that Manager as he was carrying a message from him to be delivered to his friend at Delhi. Finally, after more than an hour of struggling he could get the DD encashed.

A few anomalies in the Bank procedures are also worth noting.

A few years ago, for fixed deposits for periods ranging upto 3 months, the rate of interest was less than that allowed on the amounts in S.B. accounts.

The charges for a DD of a value of less than Rs. 500/- was Rs. 2/-. But the charges for a DD for a value of Rs. 500/- and above was Rs. 5/-. Suppose, some body takes two DDs for Rs. 300/- and Rs. 200/-, he has to pay Rs. 4/- only as the service charge. But, if he takes one DD for Rs. 500/- he has to pay Rs. 5/- as service charge. Actually, in issuing two DDs, the Bank spends more time and uses more stationary. This anomaly was so obvious. But those rates continued for a long time.

Perhaps copying the practices in a few foreign countries, the rates of interest on F.D.R.s were fixed in an absurd manner as below:

Interest on FDR for 1 year	- 10% per annum
Interest on FDR for 2 years and upto 3 years	- 11% per annum
Interest on FDR for 3 years and above	- 9% per annum

(The above figures are only indicative to illustrate the point. They may not be the actuals).

Maybe, few people would opt for FDRs for more than 3

years with such interest rates. Of course, this has been set right in the recent past.

A few Nationalised Banks have raised the minimum balance to be kept in the S.B. Accounts. One customer opened his account in a Bank much earlier. His balance in his S.B. account was less than the revised stipulation of the minimum balance. For a few months, he did not have any bank transaction. Later, he went to deposit a cheque for crediting into his account and got his pass book entries updated. To his surprise, he found that an amount of Rs. 20/- was debited to his account, as his balance was less than that stipulated as per the latest revision. The customer told that he did not know about the revision with regard to the minimum balance. But the Bank Manager told him that an announcement of the Bank revising the minimum balance to be kept in S.B. A/C was published in a newspaper and it was supposed to be seen by all its customers! He said that once a debit was shown, he had no power to remove that entry.

The customer's plea that an individual letter should have been posted to him or the earlier minimum balance should be allowed till the next transaction of the customer after the revision of the minimum balance was enforced fell on deaf ears, though there is a good logic in his plea.

The above personal experiences of a few customersmust be typical of the experience of a large number of ordinary customers like them. It is suggested that the following remedial measures may be initiated at the earliest to give the customer a better deal and a semblance of satisfaction.

(1) For opening a fresh account in any bank, by depositing cash, there should be no need for introduction by another account holder.

(2) It must be notified that there shallnot be any commission on transfer of money through M.T. In the normal course, the money remitted by M.T. will remain with the bank for at least a week before it is withdrawn. It is like a deposit on which the banks need not pay any interest. Hence the concession to the

customer is well justified. Moreover this ensures the payee to have an account with a branch of the same bank at the receiving end.

(3) The bank Managers must be instructed to ensure that a transfer of an account from one branch to another does not take more than 15 days.

(4) The Banks shall be responsible for the money to be realised from the bills presented to them except in cases where the bills are found to be invalid or not honoured. In case a bill is lost, the banks shall take responsibility for getting duplicate bills or to compensate the customers. If necessary, the bills may be sent by one bank to another by Registered post or insured letter and the charges debited to the customer.

(5) The nationalised Banks and the Institutions like Post Office, Life Insurance Corporation must realise that their main function is to serve the people at large and the customers in particular. Therefore, they should be more pragmatic in the interpretation of the rules. For instance, when a customer withdraws 50% of his own deposit in C.T.D. or premia of a L.I.C. Policy, no interest should be charged on that amount. It is indeed reprehensible for a public service organisation to pay a low rate of interest on the deposit of a customer and to earn profits by lending a part of his own money to him on an exhorbitant rate of interest. There is no difference between this and the proverbial money lender's heartless attitude. At least, the latter lends his own money and does not lend the money of the customer himself. In the case of L.I.C. Policy, the sum assured could be reduced by the amount that is withdrawn by the policy holder.

(6) If the rate of interest is altered during the course of the currency of a R.D. or a fixed deposit, either it should be applied to all schemes already started or should not be applied to any of them. But the rule should not be applied always to the disadvantage of the customer as it happened to persons mentioned above.

(7) The encashment of demand drafts should be made

easier and the customer should be spared the harassment by the Bank officers, in the name of identification. The Bank's duty should be to pay the money unless they find something wrong with the Demand Draft. Of course, the Banks could advise their customers to send crossed demand drafts, as far as possible.

(8) Provident Fund trusts and the like should be asked to pay interest until the day that the money is withdrawn by a customer and from the day an account is transferred to them. At present, these trusts have their own rules which are framed to suit their own interests. They will not pay interest for a part of the month at the time of a member joining the trust and again while leaving the trust.

(9) While giving loans to small scale industries, the condition that the entrepreneur should invest 20% of the capital should be waived. This rule is clearly favouring the richer class. If the Bank can believe a rich man and give 80% of the cost of a Project as a loan, they can surely give 100% of the cost of a Project to the poorer sections, of course, after ascertaining the viability and in very deserving cases. The loan could be given in intstalments as the work progresses.

(10) Just as the L.I.C. gives bonus to the Insurance Policy holders the banks also should give a bonus on the deposits, depending on their profits. With the rate of interest paid on savings Bank accounts and other deposits being the same in all Nationalised banks, the Banks will compete with one another by giving higher bonus to attract larger number of customers.

The Customer would feel happy if the above measures are implemented immediately and a confidential note is sent to all the staff of the Banks and other financial institutions to give up their supercilious attitude of a money lender and to be polite to the customer and make him feel important by following Mahatma Gandhi's words that "a customer is a most important visitor on the business premises and he is doing a favour by his visit."

23

Travails of the People and Government's Apathy

The Narasimha Rao Government is never missing an opportunity to give publicity to the so-called benefits derived from the liberalisation of its industrial and economic policies. However, it should be noted that the lion's share of these benefits is going to the rich people only.

Realising this, when some people made an outcry, though feeble and belated, about the lack of human face to these policies, the Government announced some poverty alleviation schemes to satisfy those critics. These schemes are far too inadequate to improve the condition of the poor to any significant extent. They are also too complicated for easy implementation.

The Government seems to be more responsive to the "crore pathies" and millionaires seeking larger profits on their investments or higher remuneration for their efforts than to the poor people clamouring for just enough means for their livelihood. The present rate at which the so-called benefits are expected to "trickle" down to the poorer sections is so low that they can never hope to cross the poverty line in the foreseable future.

It should be remembered that human face alone is not sufficient. Sometimes it could hide the real intentions and attitudes. Therefore, what is actually needed is a "human heart". The policies should therefore be modified suitably for giving a far larger share of the benefits to the poor.

The Government is also claiming to have simplified the rules and procedures to cut down the bureaucratic delays in giving approvals/sanctions for setting up industries etc. But the common man is astounded at the apathy of the Governments at the centre and in States in simple matters which are causing him a lot of irritation and hardship almost everyday.

For instance, if someone shifts his residence from one place to another and applies to the Telephone Department for shifting his telephone, it is usually taking several weeks or even months for the Department to install the phone at the new address. One fails to understand the reasons for such abnormal delay. On receipt of an application, the Telephone Department should be able to disconnect the phone within a day or two and give a certificate that he is entitled to have a telephone at his new address.

On production of the certificate, the officer in charge of the area to which the telephone is required to be shifted should arrange for the installation of a phone within another two or three days. Thus, the entire procedure should not take more than a week. But, as per the present procedure, the customer is made to run from pillar to post before the phone is installed at the new address. These remarks apply to the present procedures for shifting a gas connection and changing a ration card as well.

If a power of attorney, or a lease-deed or any other document has to be registered, the applicants are given a receipt after the registration and are asked to collect the original document on a specified date after about 4 to 6 weeks. But very often, after waiting in the queue for a long time on the appointed day, the applicants return with a bitter feeling when they are told by the clerk that the documents are not yet ready and therefore they should check after another week or ten days. The Registrar's office does not seem to have any concern for the inconvenience and hardship caused to the applicants, not to speak of the time and money that they have spent in this process.

It is understandable if the Passport Department requires a lot of information about an applicant before a Passport is issued in the first instance. But, one wonders why the same details should be sought all over again when he applies for the renewal of his passport after 10 years. This procedure does not seem to be really necessary. At the most, the passport holder may be asked to affix a recent photograph, as there could be some change in his/her appearance over such a long period. The present elaborate procedure is not only causing needless delays in the issue of the renewed passports, but also increasing the work load of the Passport Department considerably. For missing new passport, the Department is taking unduly long time ranging from 6 months to a year.

Although here and there a few tenants are giving trouble to the landlords, generally it is the landlords who are harassing the tenants with the exception of a few. Many tenants are denied the refund of the Security Deposit by the greedy and highhanded landlords while vacating the houses. A few landlords are incorporating stringent conditions in the leasedeeds and are trying to implement them to the letter like Shylock. It is not easy for the tenants to go to Courts of law for justice as it is costly as well as time consuming.

The Government could stipulate a standard form of lease agreement and also nominate a person/persons in each locality to resolve the disputes between landlords and tenants expeditiously.

After the outbreak of plague in September, 1994 in some parts of the country, the Government and the people seemed to have realised the need for maintaining good sanitary conditions in the cities, towns and villages. The photographs of the garbage heaps, pools of sewage water and many other areas abounding with filth were published in many leading magazines and newspapers to draw the attention of all concerned to this health hazard. But, once the menace of plague faded away, the Government and the people seem to have forgotten their resolve to maintain the places neat and clean.

Natural calamities like cyclones, floods, earthquakes are also being tackled in the same fashion. Year after year, several lakhs of people living on the banks of the rivers and in lowlying areas are badly affected by the floods. But nothing much is done either to rehabilitate the victims at a safer place or to protect the affected areas from the fury of the floods in future. Instead of spending money on throwing crumbs to the flood victims every year, the concerned Government could do something positive to avoid recurrence of the problem. The rehabilitation should be on a permanent basis rather than on a stop-gap basis. If the low lying areas cannot be protected from submersion, people should not be allowed to construct their huts/houses in that area.

The officers responsible for demolition of unauthorised buildings are receiving a lot of praise and publicity. But is it not more important to prevent unauthorised construction in the first place? By doing so, the waste/loss of money of—whose ever it may be—involved in the demolition can be avoided. If the unauthorised buildings do not come in the way of safety and civic rules of the town, the concerned authorities should confiscate them instead of demolishing them. Stringent action should be taken on the Government/Municipal staff due to whose negligence/complicity the unauthorised buildings have been constructed.

The idea of issuing photo identity cards to the electorate was mooted in 1992. But till now, perhaps not even 50 per cent of the electorate have got them. This could be attributed partly to the defects in the procedure itself. Many people would not have noted the dates published in selected newspapers for issue of their photo identity cards. Or, on those dates, they might be busy or out of station or otherwise incapacitated to go to the specified places. Moreover, on the appointed dates, some times there are abnormal delays in commencing the work due to some reason or the other and/or the crowds are too large and all of them could not be photographed.

These defects could easily be overcome by appointing a photo studio in each locality to photograph the voters as and when they go there over a period of three to four months. If this is done, the chances of some people not getting photo identity cards can be avoided.

The above points may appear to be trivial and simple. But the amount of suffering/ mental tention caused to the common many on account of them is quite tremendous. The list given in this article is by no means exhaustive. There are many more similar points causing concern to the people.

The Governments can do a lot on these matters. The people will appreciate the simplification of these rules and procedures and instructions to the concerned departments to avoid delays in serving the people. Thereby corruption too can be reduced to some extent. The importance of this for not only giving satisfaction to the people but also for the progress of the country cannot be over emphasised.

24

Little Things to Improve the Quality of Life

There is no doubt that the quality of life has improved considerably with the advent of the industrial revolution. Science and Technology are being increasingly used for providing better amenities to the people. For an orderly and systematic development, management techniques are being applied in all fields of activity. The expression "total quality management" has acquired a great currency in the recent times. The registration of Industries and business enterprises under ISO-9000 for ensuring the quality of products and services to International standards is also considered to be a step in the right direction for giving the people their money's worth.

But, corresponding with our efforts to achieve excellence in the quality of products, should we not also give a little attention to the habits, attitudes and temperaments of the people and certain procedures in offices which have got so much to do with the quality of life?

In the daily routine of our lives, we often come across incidents that would cause a lot of irritation, annoyance, needless trouble, monetary loss and waste of time. If only the people are a little more careful about this aspect, such incidents can be minimised to a very large extent. A few instances are given below in order to elaborate this point.

Many times we feel annoyed to see the letter inside an envelope getting torn off while the envelope is being opened. This happens because while sealing the envelope, care is not bestowed to ensure that the letter placed inside would not get stuck up to the envelope. Even the Inland letters are pasted in such a manner that at times the written matter gets mutilated or obliterated while they are torn open. In most of the post offices, the customers would find that gum is not available for pasting an envelope. Even if it is there, one has to use his finger to take out the gum and he is often annoyed with such an unpleasant experience. It would not cost much for each Post Office to provide a few gum bottles with a small brush inside for the benefit of the customers. The number of such gum bottles could be decided on the size of the post office. If the officials entertain the baseless fear that they may be stolen, the bottles could be tied to the table on which they are kept. For pasting the stamps, wet sponge pads should be kept.

Some times, the parents of the students in the Schools feel irritated when they are told at the cash counter that the fee that has to be paid is more than the normal fee. They would have stood in the queue for a long time before coming to know of this. If they have not taken the extra money with them, they would have to return home and make another visit to the school for payment of the fees. If the teachers announce in the class room on the first working day of a calender month the amount that has to be paid as the fee, the parents could be spared this bitter experience. This could be even written at the top of the black boards for the students to make a note of it.

In the mutual funds of U.T.I. and nationalised banks, an offer of an incentive is usually made. This incentive ranges between 3% and 1/2% (these limits could be different also) depending on how early the subscription is made by a customer. It is stipulated that the full amount has to be paid by the subscriber without deducting the incentive offered. The incentive is paid to the customers a few months after the subscription, while sending the certificates of the units.

Anybody could see that this procedure is increasing the volume of work of U.T.I. and the nationalised Banks unnecessarily and locking up the incentive money of the customers for long durations. Issue of so many incentive cheques requires a lot of manpower and stationery. It also increases the work of the postal department and the banks to that extent. In addition, the poor customer would have to wait for several months for getting these cheques. If there is a mistake in the cheque or loss in postal transit, it leads to further correspondence. Therefore, it would be far more reasonable if the customers are allowed to make their subscription after deducting the incentive money that is offered to them.

In the O.P.D.'s of AIIMS, the cards are given to the patients from 8.00 AM. But the doctors would start examining the patients from 9.30 AM onwards only. The first patient, thus, will have to wait for a minimum of 1-1/2 hours before he is examined by the doctor. Is it not possible to change the timings of the registration so that this waiting time can be reduced? The moment, the doctor arrives, all the patients cluster in front of the door. The doctor calls the names from the room. At times, the voice is hardly audible to a patient standing a little farther away. Therefore in their anxiety to be within the ear shot, the patients jostle with one another in a congregation formed in front of the door. Sometimes, the patients get a doubt whether their cards have reached the concerned doctor's table. This is because the patient is told orally the number of the room in which he will be examined. At times, by a mistake the card is sent to another room or the patient hears the number wrongly. In either case, he waits in vain for several hours thinking that his name would be called soon. In order to avoid such a situation, a simple improvement in the procedure can be made. While noting the number of the room on the patient's card, the person at the reception/registration counter could give a small slip of a paper noting thereon the number of the room and the patient's serial number in that room. This procedure will make the patient confident that his card is sent to a particular room. He would not have to jostle in the crowd near the door as he would know as to when his turn is likely to come. If an electronic number display board is provided outside the room, it would be still better for the patients. This suggestion holds good for other hospitals also.

If you are driving a car, you would perhaps be alarmed by the attitude of many drivers. Some times, a bus may overtake your car only to stop at a busstand just in front of you, thereby forcing you to stop your car. Some car drivers behind your car might be blowing the horn impatiently knowing fully well that you cannot give way for them to overtake your car because of several slow moving vehicles plying in the lane to your left side. At times, your heart might miss a beat when you suddenly realise how narrowly you have escaped an accident when a rash youngster driving a vehicle overtook your car from the wrong side even without blowing a horn. Are not many people undergoing a lot of stress and strain on account of such incidents, daily? They are also facing the risk of meeting with accidents.

The names, addresses and details like "amounts and dates" are often written wrongly in the forms/receipts/records in offices of Insurance companies, Banks, R.T.O. offices, Railway and Airline booking offices etc. The people have good reason for getting annoyed with those offices. They also experience considerable inconvenience and sustain loss at times because of such wrong entries. If the concerned persons pay a little more attention to their work, such mistakes could be avoided, to the great relief of the customers. If the people have civic sense and concern for the health of the community, the roads, street corners, frontages of the shops and houses would not be littered with garbage and waste materials. There are many more similar things happening in almost all walks of human life. It is high time that concerted efforts are made to teach the people to be careful in whatever work they do and to improve the procedures and amenities in offices, hospitals etc. by carrying out work studies just as efforts are made to improve the quality of products. If we think that our aim is to progress towards better civilization, it is perhaps worth remembering Will Durant's words `No man who is in a hurry is civilized."

For those who believe that speed is essential for progress, these words can be modified as "Undue hurry resulting in slipshodness and tension would not be conducive to civilised and happy life".

25

Improve Civic Sense

There is no doubt that our culture, traditions and beliefs are as good as those of other countries. But, we cannot say this about our civic sense, attitudes and behaviour in public.

There is no need to admire everything that bears the stamp of a foreign country. At the same time, it is not wrong to learn a few things from some foreign countries if they are good for our society.

Now-a-days, a large number of our people are visiting foreign countries. Mostly, they comprise of Government officials, Private and Public sector Company representatives, students, cinema stars, artists, politicians, journalists and tourists. A few are going on pilgrimages too. Almost all of them extoll the good things that they have found in the advanced countries like France, Germany, England, Italy, Switzerland, Netherlands, Japan and the United States.

Many of them treat those visits as a holiday. Some others may transact some business or undergo a training or attend a seminar or visit a trade fair, besides enjoying a holiday. But invariably, all of them would bring something or other of the foreign make like a watch, a camera, a dress, a suitcase, a VCR, a scotch bottle etc. Incidentally, their status also goes up in their society.

They are also learning from the foreigners their manner isms, gesticulations such as shrugging of shoulders, rolling their eyes and sighing as an expression of surprise or disgust, a peculiar accent of some words like 'yah' for 'yes'. But they are not using their position in society or Government to educate the people and to bring about certain improvements in the attitudes and behaviour of our people to match those of the people of the advanced countries.

The politicians and Government may say that they do not have enough funds to bring the country on par with the developed countries in the near future. But the real fact is the available funds also are not utilized properly and efficiently. Therefore, we are still more backward than the excuse of lack of funds could justify. However, what is suggested here would not require large funds for implementation.

The very first thing that strikes one in the advanced countries is the cleanliness. The roads, pavements, parks and the places of tourist interest are maintained in a neat condition. The roads are free from ruts, potholes, corrugations and unevenness which are so common in our country even in cities like Delhi.

The traffic is smooth flowing because the traffic rules are observed by one and all. Buses, cars and trams are driven without causing traffic jams. The seats in those vehicels are very comfortable and always there seem to be a few vacant seats. Standing passengers are very rare.

The trains are very fast and punctual. The compartments are kept spic and span. Every long distance passenger is given a ticket bearing the coach number and seat number. The tickets can be purchased not only at the Railway stations but also at many other places like the airports. Advance booking is generally not required. At most of the Railway stations, escalators are provided.

The menace of beggars is almost nonexistent. In some

countries like France a few beggars can be seen near the tourist places like the Eiffel tower, the Leuvre etc. But they are very few and would not pester the visitors as they do in India. The beggars in India are not only causing nuisance but are proving to be a health hazard also. They usually occupy such positions on the pavements, in the subways, at the religious places etc. that the people have to walk very close to them while going from one place to another. Most of those beggars carry deadly diseases and the danger of the unwary people being affected by those diseases is indeed very great.

The pedestrians seem to be well disciplined in the advanced countries. They walk on the pavements and cross the roads only at the pedestrian crossings. They make use of the subways and overbridges wherever they are available for crossing the road. They do not obstruct the free flow of the traffic. In India we find people crossing the roads anywhere and some of them even jump over the iron grill dividers at the centre of the roads. One cannot find cattle, pigs, stray dogs, donkeys etc. on the roads of their cities unlike in India. The traffic signals are clear and easy to follow. Bill boards are prominently displayed alongside the roads indicating the distance of the next town, petrol pump, hotel etc. for the guidance of the motorists. For stopping a vehicle on the road side; refuges are provided at regular intervals on the express ways. In our cities, the pavements are not cleared of encroachments, hawkers, beggars etc. Even if some people want to keep the parks etc. clean, they can't do so as there are no dustbins provided at many places.

If our Government, local bodies and traffic police make a determined effort, the condition of the roads and traffic control can be improved without much expenditure.

The petrol pumps are installed in such a manner that any petrol pump can be reached even when all the other pumps are engaged. In India most of the petrol pumps at a filling station are located in a series causing inefficiency in their operation. For instance, if three pumps are in a row, usually the cars at the second and the third pump are delayed till the car at the first pump goes. At times, the first pump may have to be idle as a car cannot reach it, till the cars at the second and third pump are driven away. But, if the three pumps are located parallelly, any pump is accessible irrespective of the other pumps being engaged.

Similarly we find long queues of cars, buses and lorries at many checkposts and toll gates in India. The people in Europe are spared the ordeal of wasting a lot of time in such queues. At the borders between the countries, usually 15 to 20 gates are provided in parallel depending on the intensity of traffic. As a result, it would not take more than five minutes for a vehicle to cross the toll gate.

The buses, trains and trams are provided with doors which are closed through a central control system, when they are in motion. Long distance buses are provided with toilets. Pessengers travelling on the foot boards of the buses cannot be seen in those countries.

For the convenience of the people, public toilets are maintained by the city administration. An attendant is posted at every toilet block. The toilet can be used by anyone on payment of the equivalent of Rs. 10/- to Rs. 15/- in those countries. Those toilets are provided with good sanitary fittings and are kept very clean.

At the banks, tourist offices, Railway stations etc, people wait in a queue in an orderly manner. When the concerned official is attending to one customer, the next person in the queue stands at least six feet away. In India, not only the people do not stand in a queue properly, but also quite often they distrub the official by asking questions even while he is attending to another person at that time. Such cross talks any where will divert the attention of the people concerned resulting in confusion and inefficiency. It is a pity that our people lack the patience and good sense in such situations.

In those countries where a repair work is in progress on the road or pavement, that portion is well barricaded and a 'caution' board is displayed on all sides of the barricade. In India, we find that these precautions are not followed at many places. Indeed, many times manholes are left open on the roads and pavements, thus causing several accidents. Whenever, a trench is cut across a road here for laying a pipe or a cable, the same is never filled up properly. At every such location, the motorists are caught unaware till they feel a jolt while crossing the trench. Not only this results in discomfort but also this causes unnecessary wear and tear on the tyres, shock absorbers etc.

The items sold in their shops are known for their high quality. The workers may strictly follow the timings of their duty. But they give their best attention to the quality aspect. The owners of the factories and the business people may aim at making high profits. But they do not achieve their goal by sacrificing the quality. In fact, they cannot afford to ignore quality in their products in view of the stiff competition they have to face from several others manufacturing and selling those products.

In many of the European countries when the local people see a visitor from outside, they accost with a smile or a nod of their heads. Strangers in those countries form a good impression of those countries on noticing such simple gestures of warmth and friendliness.

The motorists seem to be cautious while driving near pedestrian crossings. When they find pedestrians trying to cross a road at a pedestrian crossing, often they stop their vehicles and allow the pedestrians to cross the road. The rash behaviour of the motorists and drivers of other vehicles in our country is in total contrast to that mentioned above.

In some countries like Belgium, the citizens are required to cast their votes in an election, compulsorily. Anybody who fails to vote without a valid reason is liable for a penalty. In our country also, some procedure should be devised to improve the voter turn-out in the elections to make the elections more representative and meaningful. However, levying penalty for failure to vote is not advisable. First of all, the Government must streamline the official machinery to make it prompt in including the names of all the eligible voters in the voters' lists by updating them periodically. The concerned officials must visit the residential areas in their jurisdiction atleast once in six months and enlist the new comers and delete the names of those who have left the place. It should not be necessary for the citizens to run form pillar to post to get their names included with the help of ration cards etc.

In India we find that prohibition policy varies from a State to State. Even within a State also, this policy changes often with the changes in the Government. The implementation of the prohibition policy is very difficult. The habitual drunkards are getting the liquor in some way or the other. This policy is depriving the States of a handsome revenue and helping the smugglers and illicit liquor manufacturers to thrive.

In the advanced countries, liquor is available everywhere. Bars are run like hotels and restaurants. But, there, it is rare to find a drunkard causing nuisance in public. Therefore, in India too, it is advisable to lift the prohibition. However stringent law should be enacted to punish the drunkards causing nuisance in public. In this respect, the social organisations should be activated to discourage the people from getting addicted to the habit of drinking.

It is not intended here to give a clean chit to everything happening in those countries. Corruption, crime, immorality and exploitation are rampant in those countries also. But surely, a common man is happy in his day to day life because of better facilities available, disciplined behaviour of the people and freedom from pollution.

26

Fair Deal to Salaried Employees

Most of the advertisements for posts in private and public limited companies state that attractive fringe benefits will be given in addition to salary. Some of these benefits, also termed as perks include Provident Fund, Gratuity and superannuation Fund, Medical Reimbursement and Leave Travel Assistance. But people are not aware that many of the employees feel cheated when they are denied these benefits on some pretext or the other. It is about time that the present rules governing these benefits are reviewed and rationalised so that all the employees receive their share of these benefits without having to depend on the whims and fancies of the employer.

Provident Fund

Under this scheme each employee contributes a certain percentage of his/her salary towards his/her provident fund and an equal amount is contributed by the employer. This amount bears an interest of about 9% per annum. The amount thus accumulated with interest is paid to the employee on his/her retirement or remaining unemployed for six months. This is really a laudable scheme but for the following draw-backs.

(1) What with the high rate of inflation, the value of the accumulated fund (in terms of purchasing power) at the time of retirement of an employee will be only a fraction of the value of the money at the time of its deposition.

(2) Only a certain percentage of the employer's contribution will be paid to an employee (the percentage depending on the span of the employee's membership of the Provident Fund), unless the employee/ has been a member of the Provident Fund for atleast 15 years.

(3) Withdrawals from the fund, limited to the amount contributed by an employee are permitted only for specific purposes, namely.

(i) his/her daughter's marriage.

(ii) purchase of a house plot or a house, and

(iii) treatment of serious diseases.

If this Scheme were to be truly beneficial to the employees, the following changes have to be incorporated in the rules:

(1) The PF amount at the credit of every employee should be appreciated once a year taking into account the extent of inflation that has taken place during the preceding year. This will ensure that an employee at his/her retirement will get an amount which would have the purchasing power of the money he/she would have normally got, if no inflation has occurred during the period of his/her membership of the Provident Fund.

(2) The full amount of the employer's contribution towards an employee's Provident Fund should be paid to the employee irrespective of the period for which the employee has been a member of the Provident Fund.

(3) Withdrawals by the employees should be permitted for other purposes like:

(i) children's education, and

(ii) investment in shares or business.

Gratuity

The gratuity law covers only the employees drawing a salary of less than Rs. 1000/- per month. Recently the employees drawing a salary of upto Rs. 1600/- per month also have been brought under the purview of this law. Some employers of retrograde outlook are excluding officers drawing less than Rs. 1000/- per month also from the purview of the Gratuity law taking advantage of defective wording in the law. The employees drawing more than Rs. 1000/- per month and the officers are also paid gratuity in some companies according to their own rules which vary widely from one another.

Some companies pay gratuity to their employees only if they complete a service of ten years. Some other companies stipulate even a longer period like 15 years of service for the employees to qualify themselves for receiving gratuity.

Quite often, employees are required to choose between leaving a job without gratuity for better prospects in career and remaining in the same job just to become eligible for the payment of gratuity. What-with the present rates of inflation and taxation, the savings in the salaries of even those in higher echelons will not be more than what can be termed as marginal. Therefore, even such employees feel the pinch when they are denied gratuity, applying the unreasonable rules of the companies. If it is believed that any company gets enough returns from an employee only in a long service of ten or fifteen years to justify payment of gratuity, examples are not wanting to prove that there are many who have rendered a far more useful service to a company in a shorter time than others in a much longer period. The length of service of an employee does not necessarily reflect his/her loyalty to the company either. It is common knowledge that quite a few employees opt to remain in their jobs as either they cannot get better jobs elsewhere or they are quite happy in their jobs because of ease in work or nearness to their home town or convenience for their children's education. In view of the above and with a view to extending the benefits of gratuity to all sections of the employees, the following amendments should be made to the Gratuity Act.

(1) Gratuity should be paid to all sections of employees compulsorily irrespective of the length of their service.

To lessen the financial burden on the employers, perhaps for the purpose of computing gratuity payable to an employee, the maximum salary may be taken as Rs. 15,000/- only even if an employee's salary is more than Rs. 15,000/- per month.

Medical reimbursement rules also very widely from one company to another. By complicating the rules, the companies are increasing the work load on their accountants and making their employees resort to dishonest ways to draw the amount that they are eligible for. The beneficiaries in the process are medical practitioners, chemists and druggists.

For instance, the rules of one company for medical reimbursement are as follows:

(a) Medical expenses incurred by an employee on self, his/her spouse and three children of age not exceeding 19 years will be reimbursed by the company upto a maximum of Rs. 2,400/- per annum.

(b) The medicines shall be purchased on the prescription of registered medical practioners only.

(c) The bills for the consultation fees and purchase of medicines shall be produced while claiming reimbursement of the expenses and

(d) The unspent amount, if any, is accumable for a period of three years at the end of which it will lapse.

In the above rules, the following lacunae are too glaring for any one to miss. First of all, why should all medicines be bought only with the prescription of a medical practitioner? The medicines for common ailments are quite well known and harmless. As such, why should not the employees be permitted to buy medicine directly? If the reimbursement scheme is extended only to a few of an employee's family, what about the other dependants like aged parents and children crossing the age of 19 years?

Reimbursement

In some cases, the cost of transport, nourishing food and expenses of the attendants of a patient will be much higher than the cost of medicines and Doctor's fees. Why should not these expenses also be included for reimbursement? For certain ailments like a sprain, a fracture or a scorpion bite, people have greater confidence in the treatment given by native doctors. But their bills cannot be produced for reimbursement. Doctors are invariably charging very high fees for consultation and treatment when they know that the patient/client can get reimbursement of his/her medical expenses. Supposing an employee needs a larger amount than he/she is eligible for a year, the same is not allowed even if a substantial amount would have lapsed in the preceding three years when the employee and members of his/her family would have enjoyed good health. This is really anomalous.

Therefore, it would be worthwhile to pay a certain amount as a medical allowance to an employee and leave it to him/her to spend the amount in any way he/she likes. By this, the malpractices that are going on can be put an end to and the work load on the concerned Accountants/Administrative staff of the companies can be minimised.

Leave Travel Assistance

Some employees are denied the benefit of leave travel assistance if they leave the service of a company in the middle of an year. For instance, if an employee is entitled to receive a certain amount as leave trave assistance after completing a service of one year, it is only appropriate that a proportionate amount is paid for the duration of his/her service in the year of his/her leaving the company.

Encashment of Unavailed Leave

The benefit of the encashment of unavailed leave at the end of each year may also be extended to the employees to alleviate their financial problems resulting from the ever rising cost of living. This scheme is already existing in a few organisations and if it is extended to all the organisations the vast majority of employees presently not covered by this scheme would also reap the benefit.

It can hardly be denied that companies are flourishing because of the hard work and expertise of their employees. But unfortunately, the majority of them is given a raw deal at the time of their leaving the service of the companies. It is high time that the Government should look into the above and amend the rules to remove the anomalies and to ensure justice and a fair deal to all the employees.

Note: This article was written in 1985. Since then, several improvements were made in the service conditions of salaried employees. But still the spirit of this article is relevant to their problems as of today, also.

salaried employees - at any rate an overwhelming majority of them who depend on the income from their salaries only - are hard pressed for money to make both ends meet. The income for one year is taken into consideration for assessing the tax liability of salaried employees. But, quite often, some salaried persons remain unemployed for several months or even years after having worked with a fairly good salary for some period. This could happen due to many reasons like the employees being given their jobs on a contract basis for a period of, say, three to five years only. The employers might retrench the services of some employees as the work load has decreased or business has slumped or a project is completed and the next project has not yet been taken up. Sometimes, the employees might resign due to lack of congenial atmosphere of work. The employment could also be terminated on medical and/or disciplinary grounds.

In these cases, the salaried persons might have paid incometax during the period of their employment. But, when they are unemployed and their income has come down to almost a pittance, no help comes from any quarter including the Government. In fact, it is not known why the Government should take a period of one year as a unit for the assessment of income-tax. Why should this not be, 2 or 3 years instead of one year? In these types of cases, will the Government come to the rescue of the people by at least refunding the income-tax collected from them in the earlier years?

It is only the salaried people whose income is taxed effectively at source. The income of the very affluent businessmen, traders, industrialists, land lords, cinema stars and private practitioners like architects, chartered accountants, lawyers and doctors is quite often, being successfully hidden. The tax these classes of people are paying is only perhaps a fraction of what should be paid according to the law/income-tax rules. Such tax evasions have become very rampant and perhaps 95% of such tax evaders are going scotfree. Even if a

27

Income Tax on Salaried Class

It is a well known fact that the people in the salaried class are carrying out most of the day-to-day work in all the departments of the Government, public sector companies and private sector companies. Their overall contribution to the development of the country is indeed quite substantial. Most of them slog through the best part of their lives and find themselves faced with a bleak future with hardly enough means left for their livelihood by the time they retire from service. Getting a job after retirement is very difficult. Even if they secure a job, the salary offered may be too low and their health may not be good enough for doing work for long hours.

In view of the above, the levy of income tax on salaried employees appears to be very unreasonable. Therefore, the Government should consider scrapping the incometax on Salaried employees forthwith. By doing so, the Government can take credit for benefiting a few lakhs of Salaried employees. People will appreciate the Government for such a progressive measure.

Government should take the following reasons and examples into consideration, while formulating the tax proposals in the next budget. With the high prices of all commodities and ever-increasing inflation in the country, the few of them are caught for tax evasion now and then, they are fighting it out in courts of law and in many cases, they are being let off for want of acceptable proof. Similarly, the illegal income of the corrupt people and smugglers etc. is not being taxed as there is no record for such income.

The income tax is levied on the basis of an individual's income for an assessment year without taking into account the factors like the size of the individual's family, his/her commitments, his/her age, the place of employment etc. Of course, this is not easy and is quite cumbersome. However, let us consider how important these criteria are as in the following examples. One salaried man has got his wife, three school-going children, old parents and a grand parent to support. His salary has just reached Rs. 48,000/- per annum. Will he be able to make both ends meet with his salary in a place like Delhi? Is there justification for levy of income-tax in this case, simply because his salary has exceeded the exemption limit?

Let us take another example. One salaried employee has slogged for more than 25 years without crossing the exemption limit for income tax. The salary being low, all these years, his/her savings are negligible. The exployee gets a raise in salary when he/she is due for retirement within a very short period and thus comes into the category of income-tax payers. Is it fair to levy income-tax on such a person and deprive him/her of the meagre chance of saving a bit for his/her retired life?

In yet another example, a person might have remained unemployed for several years and borrowed a lot of money for his/her sustenance. Then, the person gets an employment for a duration of only three years with a salary of Rs. 60000/- per annum. Is it just for the government to burden such a person with the income-tax? He/she has not only to repay the debts but also has to contend with an uncertain future after the specific period of employment.

Some persons may have to spend a lot of money on medical

care (even more than their eligibility for reimbursement), or for travel to satisfty a desire of self or dependants to see places of pilgrimage or to pursue certain hobbies like writing, painting and photography. Should a salaried person with no additional income be fleeced with income-tax and denied that little extra money which could otherwise be used for any of the above mentioned purposes?

It is laudable that the non-resident Indians are exempted totally from income-tax although they enjoy the advantages denied to salaried employees in the category of resident Indians. For the same work, the salary paid in foreign countries is far higher than in India. They can buy a lot of articles like V.C.Rs, stereo cassettee players, watches, computers, fancy clothes etc. which are the envy of the resident Indians. They are also getting special concessions for investment of their money in India, as they are earing foreign exchange for the country. The least that the salaried employees of the category of resident Indians expect from the Government is to do away with the tax on their income from their salaries.

The net amount that the Government is realising through income tax on Salaried employees is perhaps not very large if the administrative charges for collecting it are taken into account. The income-tax forms are so complicated and the rules are changing so often that an average salaried employee has to get the help of a tax consultant for filling up the form, by paying a fee.

In view of the above, the Government should consider the plight of the vast majority of the salaried employees and give them relief by scrapping the income-tax on their salaries in toto. The Government can easily make up for this loss by adopting stiffer measures for collecting taxes from the affluent section and levying higher taxes on posh and highly valuable properties and itmes of fancy art collections etc. Even otherwise, the loss on account of scrapping the income tax can easily be absorbed by the Government by pruning the extravagance in their spending in some areas. The scrapping of the income tax on the salaries of the people should be treated like the other progressive schemes for the needy, like writing off bank loans of the poor farmers and subsiding the supply of food grains to the weaker sections.

(*Note*: This chapter was written much before the 5th Pay Commission had submitted its report. It appears that some categories of the Govt. employees are now going to get fabulous salaries. Salaries of more than Rs. 20,000 per month per person may be suitably pruned down while giving exemption from the levy of income tax.)

28

The Ancient Mariner and I

I and my wife Radha entered the wedding house. The bride's father, Rajarao is my wife's uncle. He and his wife, Shyamala auntie had received us warmly and shown us to a room. Already quite a few guests had arrived and the house was bustling with activity. The decoration of the house with festoons and lights was quite pleasing. The music over the loud speaker was stirring in me sweet memories and desires.

My wife had quickly changed her dress, given a few touches to her beautiful face and looked into the mirror with satisfaction. In that yellow silk saree with dark red border, she looked as sweet and charming as on the day of our marriage. With a sudden impulse, I took her into my arms and my lips started roving on her face. "Oh! don't be naughty, you have ruined my make up". She said with mock anger struggling out of my embrace. There was a gentle knock on the door. "That should be aunty Shyamala. I have to go and help her. Till the marriage is over, I am afraid I have to leave you by yourself." She said with a bewitching smile. Before I could say anything, she opened the door and vanished along with aunty Shyamala into the room where the bride Nalini was seated.

After relaxing for a while, I went along with the other guests and finished a sumptuous dinner served by the hosts. It was then about 9.00 P.M. The marriage "muhurtam" was at 1.00 A.M. I was wondering how I should spend these four hours. Two groups of people had settled down to play cards. A few others were chatting and laughing loudly whenever some one had cut a joke. I was feeling lonely. Many of the guests were strangers to me. I am by nature, very reticent in the company of strangers, although I could be voluble in the midst of close friends or admirers.

I dismissed the idea of going to sleep, for in that case, I would surely not wake up by the "muhuratam" time. My better half would severely admonish me for such a lapse. Therefore I just went to a secluded corner, away from the "pandal" and sat on a folding chair. Looking at the starlit, cloudless sky I was hoping to get some ideas for my next story.

"Are you not Kittu, the husband of our Dharmarao's daughter, Radha?" These words woke me up from my reverie. I looked up and saw a six feet and odd hefty figure drawing a chair and sitting before me. I nodded my head and said "yes". He should be around fifty five years of age. "I am Dharmarao's cousin and my name is Govind. I have retired from the Navy just a few months ago. I have seen you at the time of your marriage, two years ago;" he said.

For the sake of politeness, I said, "Life in the armed forces must have been very exciting." My seemingly innocuous remark had brought about a sudden change in him. The smile on his face had vanished. He looked quite serious and in a sonorous tone replied, "Yes. The life in the naval force was quite exciting. I have served on the front in two wars and was hospitalised thrice due to serious injuries. I have also won an award for gallantry. I have retired from service recently. My hope was that I would be able to buy a good house and live comfortably on the pension I am to get. But, you know with the price rise, I am unable to buy even a two bed room house with the amount I got as my retirement benefit. Certain things seem to be always out of reach of the common man. Ten years ago, a 1000 square feet house was costing around Rs. 20,000 and I thought I should be able to buy a house by the time I retire. But imagine, with the Rs. 50,000 that I am getting as my retirement benefit, I am unable to buy a house of 1000 square feet with the land".

I thought I had started the wrong subject and trying to close the topic, I said, "I agree with you, uncle. Most people are reeling under the unabated price rise and inflation. The purchasing power of money is going down. I think there are few who are escaping the effects of price rise."

"No, my boy", uncle Govind resumed. "You are sadly mistaken. Only people like me who do sincere and honest work for the few chips as salary are finding it difficult to make both ends meet. You would not perhaps believe, but the popular cinema actor Ramanarao was my class mate in School. He used to act in our school dramas. With his extra curricular activities, he was never getting good marks in any subject. His father used to scold him often for his poor performance in studies. He was struggling without a permanent job for five years after leaving school. He continued to act in dramas on and off to supplement his earnings. Then he secured a small role in a picture "Satyabhama" and received encomiums for his talent. Very soon he became quite a popular actor. He is now owning three palatial bungalows and ten acres of the most fertile land. The jewellery, money and the cars in his possession are the envy of even his rich relations. His father is now an old man of about eighty years and is proud of his son. Do you think that he has rendered a more useful service to the Nation than a soldier like me or for than matter, an engineer like you?"

Lest he should think that I am not showing interest, I interceded to say "But, uncle, in the case of actors, the risk of losing their jobs is always there. The period of their earnings also is quite limited."

"You are speaking as though, in any other profession, the risk of losing a job is not there!", he cut me short. "Suppose, a patient's condition is aggravated due to the negligence of a surgeon performing an operation, is he not punished? Does he not lose his job although he would have been quite efficient in many earlier surgeries? Who does not have the fear of losing a job? But then an actor earns enough by the time he fades away in his profession, whereas any other honest employee would not have any earnings worth mentioning to depend upon, if he has to face similar circumstances."

"But, you know, the producer can afford to give the fabulous fee to the actors as he also gets good returns from his film", I interjected, wondering what might be the reaction of uncle Govind to these words.

"Ah! That is how people explain away the payment of unreasonably high amounts to the actors", Uncle Govind admonished. "Why should they charge such high fares from the cine goers? Why can't they cut the cost of production of each film by reducing the fabulous fee to each actor, actress and other artistes and reduce the ticket price for cinemas so that millions of cine goers can get a little relief? Do you think that the best of the actors is more talented than the best of the administrators, doctors, engineers, soldiers and scientists?" Do you think that the so called "talented actors" would cease to be actors if their rates are cut down to say Rs. 10,000 per film, if they are paid Rs. 1,00,000 now? No! They would still continue to be actors. If a few of them refuse to act, thousands of others equally talented would be ready to step into their shoes, at the reduced rates as I have told. This is one class of people who are not much bothered by the price rise. There are, of course, many other classes of people like the one I have mentioned, who are growing rich out of proportion due to the patronage of the poor masses. Take, for instance, the sportsmen like cricketers, Tennis players and boxers. Once any of these and similar sportsmen reaches the State or National level, his earnings reach an astronomical figure. If a cricketer has earned Rs. 5,00,000 in a span of six years of his career and still laments that he is unable to lead a life like another in England or Australia, our poor sports fans are all sympathy for him. A cricketer scoring a hundred runs is considered a greater hero by our emotion prone masses than a General who led his army to a victory or an engineer who has to do so much design and planning in constructing a bridge or a dam across a river. Even the names of scientists in the space craft project might not be known, but the names of a cricketer who ran through his opponents' team with his in swingers, out swingers, googlies and bouncers or a fielder who got a batsman out by running ten yards, diving and holding a one handed catch or the tennis star who emerged as champion in an open tournament are remembered for years by their crazy fans. Many of the sportsmen are given lucrative jobs by some organisations as an incentive to sport.

Something in me was persuading to argue and point out what an injustice he was doing to the sportsmen. But before I could marshall my thoughts, he continued his fluent talk. "Yet another class that is thriving luxuriously without deserving it is the business community. Our banks are such that they trust the rich who could invest say 10% of the cost of a project by advancing the balance 90% of the investment as a credit. Once a business or a factory is started, the promotor or the Managing Director becomes a virtual monarch. Besides drawing fantastic salary and perquisites which are beyond the imagination of a common man, he appoints all his kinsfolk in key positions with high salaries and powers. Qualification and experience are not at all the criteria for these appointments. However if an outsider were to be chosen for any of these posts, a very high qualification and long experience are prescribed for the prospective applicants.

The bosses at helm who enjoy an easy and comfortable life exhort the poor employees lower down to work still harder and to observe greater austerity. Such exhortations from those who indulge in spending lavishly at the expense of the organisations, in expensive liquour, air travel on every pretext, entertainment etc sound quite funny. The people in this privileged class are bullies of the worst type. Not knowing even A, B, C, D of engineering, accountancy, technology or labour laws, they control engineers, accountants, technologists and liaison officers by their mere power to punish anyone who could dare to raise his voice against them. Their main aim in business is to line their pockets and build their properties by the sweat and blood of thousands of the workers, staff and officers. If an employee in service constructs a big house within five years of service, people raise their eyebrows and, may be, with justification he is branded as corrupt. But if a businessman has constructed three houses within that period, he is praised for his business acumen."

By now I was rapt with attention and I did not like to interrupt the ex-soldier's narration of his thoughts.

"The workers looked for some protection against indiscriminate punishment, victimisation and denial of share in profit for which they strove as much as their bosses. And the result is the birth of yet another class of people who by appearing to serve these poor hapless workers get themselves richer and richer, day by day".

I was unable to guess what he was driving at. Before I could ask him for clarification, he proceeded to say, "This class consists of the trade union leaders and politicians. They always pose to serve the interests of the poor. Each agitation of the workers results in substantial pecuniary gains and rise in popularity for the leaders. The agitators get a few doles for themselves after passing through a lot of suffering. In no time the trade union leaders and political leaders become members of the rich class either through the modest contributions from the people they ostensibly serve or by other means. And, mind you, it is not questioned by any one in most cases as to how an ordinary man could become so rich in such a short time if he had paid the income tax properly. In short, if any one could be proficient in any act or craft which evokes interest of a large number of people could easily make a lot of money with relatively very little effort. Take the case of a good singer or a good painter or one who is endowed with powers of oratory or writing novels. All of them put their talent to good use and succeed in making lots of money. People are told that unless they have the opportunity to make money like that, there won't be any incentive for their talents to be displayed. But I wonder how the immortal writers of the olden days had displayed their talent even though some of them like Goldsmith lived in virtual penury.

There was a time when entertainers were considered to be lower in social status. Singing and dancing in public were looked down upon and were pursued as a profession of certain castes only. Now, because of the potential for making money, they have attained the status of fine arts and are being pursued by the people of all castes. Now they constitute a part of the superior class. Sport was considered to be nothing more than a pastime. To me it makes little difference whether a man ran a mile in 3 minutes 55 seconds or 3 minutes 56 seconds as long as he is quite fast; athletic and sportive. I feel giving say Rs. 10,000 to the one who comes first and giving just Rs. 2,000 for the one who comes a close second to him as prize and nothing at all to the others is unjustified.

I don't know when people would cease to think that money is the only incentive for display of talents. Unless this trend changes the disparities cannot be reduced. Inflation is bound to increase and the salary earning people like us, the soldiers, engineers, accountants, workers and the like are destined to live our lives not far above the poverty line". Uncle Govind stopped for a breath.

Suddenly I heard the voice of my wife "I am searching for you all over the place. Where is the wedding gift? Please bring it over. The "muhuratam time is approaching." I got up from my chair, hurriedly. It appeared as though I have just now come out from a dream. I found people moving about briskly in the pandal. Lilting notes of Shehnai were enchanting the listeners. I looked at uncle Govind who seemed to be a trifle disappointed to find his listener absent.

I recalled my favourite poem "The Ancient Mariner". I thought I am now truly "a sadder and a wiser man" after listening to uncle Govind. I started thinking "why every man after a life time of service in any capacity cannot be assured a decent house and enough for him and his family to live on".